Carpets of
the Orient

Carpets of the Orient

Text by Ludmila Kybalová and Photographs by Dominique Darbois

Paul Hamlyn

London · New York · Sydney · Toronto

Text by Ludmila Kybalová
Translated by Till Gottheiner
Photographs by Dominique Darbois
Graphic design by Přemysl Pospíšil and Miroslav Rada
Designed and produced by Artia for
The Hamlyn Publishing Group Limited
LONDON • NEW YORK • SYDNEY • TORONTO
Hamlyn House, Feltham, Middlesex, England

Printed in Czechoslovakia by Polygrafia, Prague
2/99/15/51
ISBN 0 600 00645 x

Second impression 1970

Frontispiece: Carlo Crivelli, The Annunciation, with St Emidius.
The National Gallery, London.

CONTENTS

Introduction 7

Carpet Production 13

Glossary of Ornaments 16

Survey of Production Areas 26

    Iran 26

    Central Asia (Western Turkestan, Eastern Turkestan, 34
    Afghanistan, Beluchistan)

    Asia Minor 39

    Caucasus 44

    Armenia and Kurdistan 48

    China 49

    Pakistan 49

    India 50

    Japan 50

    Spain 50

    Africa (Morocco, Algeria, Tunisia, Egypt) 50

Notes for Collectors 53

List of Carpets 55

List of Illustrations 56

Map 59

Illustrations 61

The Western world always remains a little jealous of the Orient which manages to combine beauty and function, work and relaxation, ostentation and simplicity, luxury and asceticism, comfort and austerity. It admires the Oriental facility of making each object in a manner that perfectly suits all its needs yet retains some magic and mystery. The fine arts are enhanced by forms which, in Western terms, belong to the field of applied arts. In a world where all sharp dividing lines merge, these divisions lose all meaning.

In the Orient, carpets are man's constant companion. They serve his personal comfort; they adorn the sacred area where he says his prayers; they decorate his house, as couch, cover and saddle, and in the steppes provide shelter.

The Old Testament records how carpets were woven and how they were used to build tents:

And every wise hearted man among them that wrought the work of the tabernacle made ten curtains of fine twined linen, and blue, and purple, and scarlet: with cherubims of cunning work made he them.

The length of one curtain was twenty and eight cubits, and the breadth of one curtain four cubits: the curtains were all of one size.

And he coupled the five curtains one unto another: and the other five curtains he coupled one unto another.

And he made loops of blue on the edge of one curtain from the selvedge in the coupling: likewise he made in the uttermost side of another curtain, in the coupling of the second.

Fifty loops made he in one curtain, and fifty loops made he in the edge of the curtain which was in the coupling of the second: the loops held one curtain to another.

And he made fifty taches of gold, and coupled the curtains one unto another with the taches: so it became one tabernacle.

And he made curtains of goats' hair for the tent over the tabernacle: eleven curtains he made them.

And the length of one curtain was thirty cubits, and four cubits was the breadth of one curtain; the eleven curtains were of one size.

And he coupled five curtains by themselves, and six curtains by themselves.

And he made fifty loops upon the uttermost edge of the curtain in the coupling, and fifty loops made he upon the edge of the curtain which coupleth the second.

And he made fifty taches of brass to couple the tent together, that it might be one.

And he made a covering for the tent of rams' skins dyed red, and a covering of badgers' skins above that.

And he made a veil of blue, and purple, and scarlet, and fine twined linen: with cherubims made he it of cunning work.

And he made an hanging for the tabernacle door of blue, and purple, and scarlet, and fine twined linen, of needlework.

Exodus XXXVI, 8-19, 35, 37

This passage shows that in antiquity carpets were used both on the floor and as covers and wall hangings, corresponding to the Latin word *tapete*. Apart from the carpet's practical function during the building of Solomon's temple, as described in Exodus, it was clearly regarded as a precious artifact. On an Assyrian relief in the British Museum of the time of Shalmaneser III (859—824 B.C.), there is a scene showing a ruler receiving several precious gifts, among them a carpet. On the Apis statue in the Louvre the god is depicted in full decoration, which includes a carpet on his back. The divan on which Cleopatra was said to have gone to meet Anthony was draped with precious carpets.

I, II Carpet found in Pazyryk, southern Siberia.
Whole carpet and
detail

I, II Carpet found in Pazyryk, southern Siberia.
Whole carpet and
detail

Although carpets are part of the comfort of everyday Oriental life, their
utilitarian functions do not deprive them of their artistic qualities. Their value
is the obvious result of complex decoration, precious materials and the inherent
worth of a craft, which has been carried on and developed through the work of
centuries. Research shows that carpets are formed by a highly involved evolutionary relationship between a variety of materials, regional peculiarities and
a wealth of symbols. Carpet-making is an art form which, legend relates, the
Muslim scholar Lokman learnt from a spider through whose net flows the holy
water of the Ganges.

The territory of present-day Iran (Persia) formed the cradle of the art of
knotting and weaving carpets. The Assyrian relief mentioned above is the earliest
evidence of the use of carpets. The oldest existing carpets, dating from the fifth
to fourth centuries B.C., have recently been found in the Altai region, and in
eastern Turkestan.

A carpet, now in the Hermitage Museum, Leningrad, was found preserved by ice
in the tomb of an Altai prince in Pazyryk in southern Siberia (see figs. I and II).
Investigations suggest that it is of Persian origin; the decorative motifs are
similar to those of the Achaemenian period. Apart from its dense, regular
structure, the composition is surprisingly 'classical' although the square shape
is rather unusual for an archaic work. The inner field is divided into regular
chess-board squares filled with star rosettes surrounded by a five-part border
pattern alternating men on horseback with stripes of lotus and rosettes. The
perfect balance of the design and the precision and purity of execution indicate
that it is not an isolated work, but must have been the result of a long tradition.

Before the discovery of the Altai tomb the oldest carpet known was that of
the Sassanian king, Chosroes I (A.D. 531—579). Its existence is a matter of
legend since it only survives in a number of copies, and through descriptions in
poetry. The carpet was used by the king in winter to remind him of spring-

time garden in blossom. Woven in gold, silver and silk, it had a design of a garden, with paths and streams. Fruit and flowers were picked out by precious stones against the golden earth. Very little is known about the production of such carpets and none have survived. The development of workshops in the Persian provinces of Khuzistan and Fars is also a mystery, but some pre-Christian records do exist for the towns of Sidon and Tyre in Asia Minor. From the third century A.D. onwards carpet-making spread to the whole of the Orient. Marco Polo, that observant commentator, mentioned flourishing production in the thirteenth century.

In the Middle Ages carpets brought to Europe from the Orient an aura of mystery and magnificence. They decorated the walls of churches on holidays and were placed on the steps before the main altar, separating the altar from the faithful. Just as in medieval paintings of the Madonna and Child the carpet placed below the throne separates the Virgin from terrestial things, and at court the carpet below the throne acted as dividing line between the ruler and his courtiers. Joinville recorded a noteworthy occasion when Saint Louis of France had a carpet spread in his garden and invited all his courtiers to sit on it. Under the Bourbons no one was allowed to step on the carpet unless ordered to do so by the king himself. Even Louis XIII as a seven-year-old prince was careful to make sure, during a reception of a Turkish ambassador, that his guest did not tread upon the carpet. Some carpets had royal symbols woven into their centre. During the stormy history of France, the Bourbon emblems had to be replaced by those of the Republicans, then by Napoleon's and later back again to the Bourbons', and many carpets were ruined as a result.

European paintings, especially Italian and Dutch, provide better evidence of the use of carpets than documents do. The great detail included in many of these works means that it is usually possible to determine the country or area of origin of the carpet shown, and also the function it played. Venetian paintings provide evidence of the first occasion European fashions were influenced by the Orient and show scenes of Venetian festivities with carpets hanging from the balconies. Venice was unusual in having particularly close relations with the Orient, but the rest of Europe also sought their carpets. In the still-lifes and interiors of the golden age of Dutch painting valuable Oriental carpets frequently cover tables loaded with heavy tableware, fruit and wine.

In a Persian house carpets have traditional and specified places.* In European, and later American collections they adorn interiors built in the European style and assume a new significance and a novel function.

The attitude towards originality in art has in the past been very different from what it is today. Just as the traditions of the Gothic Madonna are accepted, Oriental carpets with identical basic designs were not thought to be plagiarisms or imitations. They were based on traditional designs and fixed methods of craftsmanship with a vast variety of individual regional differences.

In the twentieth century these traditional and regional characteristics started disappearing. Popular Persian designs and precious historical pieces began to be produced on a large scale in Asia Minor in particular, and elsewhere; they were mass-produced mechanically, without any sort of craftsmanship. The collectors who, without being directly responsible, largely contributed to this decline found it increasingly difficult to obtain carpets for their collections. Many of the examples of the last one hundred and fifty years must be considered valueless modern productions.

The overwhelming majority of Oriental carpets forms part of Islamic culture.

---

* In the centre of the room lay the **Mian Farsh,** a rectangular carpet about 5 to 6 m. long and 1.80 to 2.50 m. wide. At each side there lay two smaller runners **Kenareh,** 1 m. wide and of the same length as the **Mian Farsh.** Diagonally placed lay the main carpet, **Kellegi,** 3 to 3.60 m. long and 1.50 to 1.80 m. wide (see figure VII, p. 12).

This one fact explains many of the peculiarities and the strange features of their style. The Arabs were in many ways very tolerant as conquerors; they left important duties of administration to the local population and permitted them to go on speaking their own language. While they imposed their religion upon the countries under their sway, it did not have a specific artistic form. As a result, art continued to develop along local lines and only gradually became a form common to all Islam. Egyptian and Coptic craftsmen working on the construction of mosques applied, as late as the thirteenth century, elements of late Hellenistic and Christian art.

In the course of time the Muslims found adequate forms of artistic expression for their religion in the cultures of Byzantium and Persia, into which they frequently introduced Hellenistic features. In foreign countries anything that survived was adapted. Hence the local differences found in Oriental carpets are contained within a framework of Islamic culture.

Different though the patterns on Oriental carpets are, and though individual motifs pass with minor variations from region to region acquiring new meaning, it is possible to set down certain general principles of decoration. Every motif, plant, animal or elementary geometrical figure, is an embodiment of a higher order. The motifs are not taken from nature, but are drawn from a system of ornamental composition. Plants do not have natural forms, but are adapted into circles, spirals and arches. No emotion is expressed, the only concern is a rich rhythmical repetition covering the whole area of the carpets.

Geometrical forms and strictly symmetrical designs became the moving force for Islamic artists in the same way as Europeans used nature. The plants on carpets are either stylised or fantastic, and can only rarely be recognised. The wide variety of shapes, in fact, have their origins in only a few prototypes; most frequent are Byzantine acanthus, palmette or vine leaves. Local flora does not occur at all. Any illusion of a third dimension is practically entirely absent, the patterns are flat and cover the whole area without any restful space. The constant merging of reality and imagination in Muslim art makes appreciation and understanding the more difficult. Since the artist did not portray nature directly, he revealed a great deal more about his inner life than about his surroundings.

III Jan van Eyck, *Madonna of Canon van der Paele,* 1436, Bruges

The scenes of fighting animals or hunting are not illustrations of real contests; they are simply a repetition of older patterns of Assyrian, Egyptian or Byzantine origin; they contain symbolic meaning and serve decorative functions.

It is far from easy to characterise individual kinds of Oriental carpets. What can be said of one group applies with minor changes to others and yet each carpet is a unique work of art in itself.

The Chinese attitude to nature was rather different from that just described. Chinese artists observed closely and drew repeatedly until they could embody the essence of each object in the simplest forms. Chinese carpets are more naturalistic. The quiet, empty background plays an important part in their design and the plastic cut of the pile, making the pattern stand out, increases the effect of naturalism.

The most imaginatively stylised patterns appear in Persian carpets, especially those designed to enhance the magnificence and splendour of the royal court and made in court workshops. Many do not contain a single realistic flower, but surpass nature in their richness and exuberance.

The most strictly geometrical in design are Caucasian carpets, mostly the work of nomads, whose harsh life made them turn, even in decoration, to simple forms. Their narrow looms, restricted range of colours and the looser texture than many more luxurious carpets conditioned the simple, geometrical shapes, animal and floral forms of great economy. Their often ingenious condensation lends them quite unexpected wealth of expression.

Islamic doctrine forbade the representation of human beings and animals. Although the Koran itself does not contain an express prohibition, Islamic scholars based on the words of Mohammed the doctrine that artists would suffer punishment if they attempted to imitate God by acts of creation. This commentary probably dates from the time of the Abbasid dynasty, a period when the words of the Prophet began to be recorded. The origin of the opposition to any depiction of human beings can be traced back, however, to an earlier period. In Syria there were earlier signs of a departure from the representation of human beings and realistic portrayal; and the Arabs themselves, before the adoption of Islam, did not worship human gods, but trees and stones. On the walls of Christian churches the sacred stories are portrayed for didactic purposes; in Islam art needs fill no such function: the dogma of Islam is simple to understand. Occasionally, human figures do occur, for example, in ancient Persian carpets and in a highly stylised form in Caucasian ones.

IV Jan Vermeer van Delft, *The Sleeping Girl*, New York

The symbolism of Oriental carpets is not limited to a certain nation or territory, but is of general application. It regulates the division of the carpet itself. The area is divided into the zemîn (background), a space that symbolises all being, and the zemân, which means 'time' or 'life', a pattern which brings the background to life. The entire compositional scheme is subjected to established norms which are never interfered with and are repeated without change.

The most common scheme, found on the majority of luxury carpets, is a medallion dividing the area into a central field and a border. The central motif, or medallion, appears in the middle of the inner field and a quarter of it is repeated in each corner. The border, which is narrow in older carpets, is split up into a varying number of strips, each of which bears a different form of decoration. In the carpets made by nomads there is the same division of central field and border, but the inner field is divided into crosswise or lengthwise strips with repetitive, regularly laid-out motifs (see fig. VI, p. 12); sometimes smaller motifs are freely scattered over the central field.

Weavers never planned the pattern of the carpet precisely in advance; they simply followed a basic scheme and filled in the details according to their own choice from the traditional repertoire of patterns. Study or classification of the endless wealth of motifs that Oriental weavers had at their disposal involves tracing an immense range of traditions. Old Egyptian motifs were mixed with

V Arrangement of carpets
   in a Persian house
VI Scheme of carpet with
   medallion
VII Scheme of prayer carpet

motifs derived from Babylon, Persia, Byzantium and Greece, which were changed by local weavers and added to new themes. Much of the main areas of carpet production have seen widespread migrations and, in any case, many carpet makers are nomads, so pattern and traditions are carried about, spread from place to place, constantly being altered. Apart from elementary geometrical figures (swastikas, meanders, rosettes, stars) floral designs are common (palmettes, arabesques, tendrils, trees, flowers) and animal shapes (animals, birds, animals fighting or hunting). Inscriptions (which either give details of the time of origin or producer, or serve merely decorative purposes), sometimes occur, and a mixture of various motifs of symbolical meaning (*chintamani*, *chi*, cloud-bands, *herati*, *gul*; see *Glossary of Ornaments*, p. 16).

Symbolical significance was also attached to the permanency and to the deep, shiny intensity of the colours. Made from natural dyes, their fastness was not only a natural result of solid craftsmanship but had also a higher significance. If the prayer rug did not have fast colours, the prayers said on it would not be of lasting quality either. Meaning was attached to particular colours: green was the colour of the Prophet, the colour of his banner, born in the struggle against the unbelievers. But green rarely appears in carpets for the foot of a believer must not come into contact with it. Blue, the colour of the air and of eternity, was used widely.

The work of the weavers was closely linked with their religion and its commandments. The closest expression of the link between carpets and religion is found in many prayer mats which every Muslim uses five times a day while saying the prescribed prayers facing towards Mecca.

The partition and layout of the prayer carpet was established by religious commandments. The design of the carpet is made in the form of an arch, whose point is turned towards Mecca during prayers (see fig. VII). Above the arch is a small diamond-shaped lozenge, woven into the pattern; on this a piece of soil or a pebble from Mecca is placed. Sometimes hands are woven into the design along the side of the lattice, in the place where the worshipper touches as he bows down. He is expected to cleanse himself before praying, so the nomad, who can only cleanse himself symbolically in the desert using sand, sometimes has a jug of water and a comb woven into his carpet.

Materials

The materials used in the production of Oriental carpets are wool, cotton, silk, linen, hemp and jute in a variety of combinations.

Wool, from sheep, camels or goats, appears in quality varying from short and wiry strands to fine, long, shiny ones, depending upon the area where the sheep are bred and the parts of the animal's body from which it is shorn, as well as on the way it is treated. Wool is used predominantly for the pile of the carpet, though some nomad carpets are made of pure wool. These often make use of the wool's natural colours, shades of white and yellow to brown, grey and black.

Cotton is a cheaper, firmer material; in the past the nomads prepared it by hand; today it is treated in numerous factories all over the Orient. It is used both as weft and warp to strengthen the carpet and prevent waviness.

Silk is one of the oldest of the luxury materials, capable of high gloss and, through its fine structure, providing for great density of structure. Silk carpets were first made in the fifteenth and sixteenth centuries in the court factories of Persia. Later, silk was used mainly for the weft.

Linen, hemp and jute, materials long in use, were employed, chiefly among nomads, as the warp and occasionally to bind the weft.

Dyes

As in the case of other crafts, the use of natural dyes, imported or of local origin, came to an end in the middle of the nineteenth century when chemical dyes began to spread to the Orient. Their use was not prevented by a law passed by the government of Persia forbidding the import of chemical dye-stuffs, nor by decrees halting production in factories where it was used. The punishment of the guilty by the loss of the right hand was soon forgotten and after the First World War the use of chemical dyes was widespread. At first the discovery of chemical dyes caused a great decline in the rich colours of Oriental carpets, but now a large number of good quality synthetic dyes are available.

Plant dyes, however, had a number of qualities which cannot be replaced. Although carpets dyed naturally lose some of their intensity of colour, they are never over bright, they age pleasantly and their tones grow softer.

The materials from which natural dyes are derived include minerals, plants and animals. Those in most frequent use are:

Red: cochineal, extracted from the kermes insect which lives in Central America and the Canary Islands. It contains scarlet. Madder dye came from a plant (*rubia tinctorum*) grown in southern Europe.

Blue: normally derived from the tropical plant indigo, or various forms of lichens and ground oak bark.

Yellow: from *bixa orellana, curcuma rotunda* and the yellow crocus (*crocus sativus*).

Green: extracted from *rhamnus chlorophorus* and from *carthamus tinctorius*.

Black: used only on very rare occasions and in small amounts, came from oak seeds or saltpetre, vinegar or the sap of the pomegranate, vinestone. When the dye was made from iron, it has often caused the wool to rot, thus the black parts of many old carpets have disintegrated.

Prescriptions for dyes remained the secret of workshops and families, handed down by each generation. Both the materials and the dyes depended on the climate and quality of the soil from which the dyes were derived. And the results also varied with the type of wool; different quality wool gives different shades even when identical methods of dyeing are used.

The material set aside for dyeing was first cleaned in hot water, sometimes with soap, to rid it of grease. Then it was soaked for twelve hours. It remained in the dye for a long time and was dried in the sun. In the factories large quantities of material were dyed at a time, but nomads could dye only small quantities at once and so they usually failed to get identical colours. One carpet, consequently, contains various shades of the same colour; this is most clearly noticeable in the background where there are larger patches of one shade.

Patterns

Nomad carpets were derived from traditional compositional schemes and motifs, and from finished carpets. They were not planned in detail in advance. Luxury carpets, however, always followed a pattern. Sketches were made by a scribe or miniaturist and transferred by draughtsmen on to draft paper with milli-metre squares, each little square representing one knot. The draft was either executed in colour, or only as a black-and-white outline with figures marking the individual colours. The draft would be cut up into strips, so that more than one man could work on the carpet at the same time. Sometimes a 'teller' would direct all the work in the place of a drawn design.

Looms

The technique of knotting carpets has not changed. It differs only according to the sophistication of the looms used. In the primitive nomad looms the warp was attached to two horizontal poles fixed to the ground on sticks; it was essential for these looms to be easily portable. The narrow, oblong shape of the nomad carpets corresponds to their comparatively narrow looms.

The vertical loom, usual in factories, was formed by two revolving cylinders connected by vertical poles. The lower cylinder held the woven carpet while the warp unwound from the upper cylinder. In the case of the more primitive looms the cylinders did not turn. During his work, the weaver constantly raised his seat, so he could see all the work he had completed. The threads of the warp were regular, stretched tightly and mostly made of undyed material. A firm edge was usually made by weaving a smooth strip, twisting the last threads of the weft, and only starting knotting when this was several centimetres wide. The knots were tied from a ball which the weaver usually had lying on the upper pole of the loom. He would begin each row of knots with two or three rows of bound weft which he then fixed firmly with a wooden or iron nail so that the carpet would be of the required density and firmness. Caucasian carpets were very often worked with the aid of a hooked knife which picked up the wool and cut it off the ball immediately. This made greater speed possible.

Today it is almost impossible to determine the number of knots that a skilled weaver was capable of tying in a day. It varies between six and ten thousand, and in the case of highly qualified craftsmen in factories it might be as much as fourteen thousand a day.

Two types of knots were used in the Orient; in Asia Minor and the Caucasus Ghiordes knots were almost exclusively used, the Persians used both Ghiordes and Sehna knots (see fig. VIII, p. 15). These European terms are derived from the traditional Persian names: *Ghiordes-aradansalma, Sehna-iandansalma*.

The finished carpet was cut so that the pile was even; this lowered it by three to six centimetres. In China it was cut in a plastic fashion, the pattern having a higher pile than the surrounding area to make it show more. After completion the carpet was washed or sprayed with water, brushed and stretched to dry.

Some older carpets which were made as insulation against cold include large numbers of two to three centimetres long woolen threads worked into the back.

Besides knotted pile carpets, *kelims*, woven carpets with patterns on both sides, were also made. These tend to be thinner and served chiefly as wall-hangings or covers. Similar looms as for knotted carpets were for the production of *kelims*. On the rare occasions when the pattern was regular stripes, the warp formed the entire width of the weft. In forming his pattern, the weaver pushed the weft very densely up to the warp to cover it entirely. Oriental carpets with a mosaic pattern occur occasionally; the design of these was made by coloured pieces of different material sewn on to the background fabric.

In the areas inhabited by nomads felt carpets were made. In Persia, central Asia, and India they were of wool, goat or camel hair, mostly in the natural colour of the wool.

VIII Scheme of Ghiordes and Sehna knots

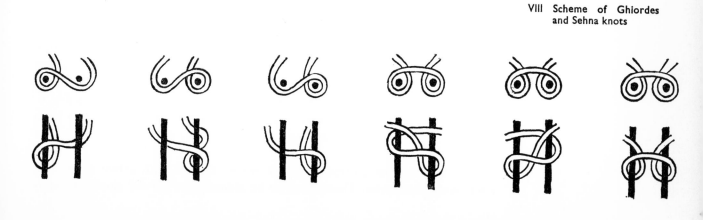

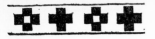

Geometrical designs

1

The **Cross** (fig. 1) has no symbolic meaning in the Orient, except in Armenia where the weavers were Christians. The most common form was the Greek cross, used horizontally or vertically in the Caucasus, and eastern Turkestan. The horizontal cross was found in western Turkestan and Yomud rugs.

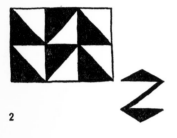

The **Triangle** (fig. 2) is the sign of happiness, the symbol of the mother of earth, of the gods; found in its simple form mainly among nomads, in more complex version in the Near East, Syria nad Morocco.

The **Chequered** design was the symbol of the sun among nomads. Originally it was a circle divided by two diagonals, but to facilitate the work of the weavers it changed into a square of equal sides – Beluchistan and Turkestan.

2

The motif of the **Swastika** (fig. 3) (from Sanscrit: *suasti* – happiness, fertility) existed from an early date in all cultures; in carpets it is used mainly on borders – India, China, Caucasus.

The **Circle** is the emblem of Buddha, who, as a small child, is said to have drawn it without having been taught to do so. Without beginning or end, it is a symbol of eternity.

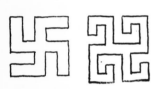

The **Diamond** (fig. 4) is a religious symbol in all Oriental carpets. It was often surrounded by outspreading rays, in fret formation.

The Jewish **Star** of King David (fig. 5), the emblem of Solomon, and the star of the Medes, are most frequently found in Soumak rugs and in the Caucasus.

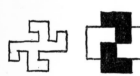

The **Octagon** (fig. 6) combined with floral motifs produced the *gul* pattern (the Persian rose), a frequent theme on Turkoman and Kara-Kirghiz carpets, and in the Caucasus. In the oases of Achal and Merv it is called the '*royal gul*'.

Borders

The **Zigzag** border (fig. 7) was the symbol of running water, which to the

3

4

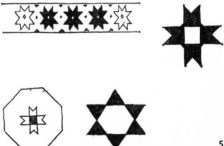

5

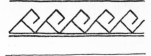

6

Egyptians meant eternity. It is also called water or wave border. Found on all types of Oriental carpets, it is particularly common in the Caucasus.

The **Meander** (fig. 8) appeared in all civilisations, but especially in China and India. Variations are **Key** and **Running-dog** borders.

Borders with the shapes of letters (fig. 9):
T – China, eastern Turkestan, Caucasus.
X, Y – Tekke (Bokhara).
S, Z – lengthwise on old Persian carpets, it symbolised light and godliness; when stylised in the shape of a serpent it symbolises human wisdom. Often found on woven Silé rugs.

Borders like a Barber's Pole (fig. 10) with different coloured spiral stripes are found on Caucasian, Persian and Turkoman carpets.

Arrow points, resembling cuneiform writing, were the emblems of the Chaldean gods, and found on Turkestan and Caucasian carpets.

Mountains and Valleys (fig. 11) occur mainly on Chinese carpets both as borders and as separate designs. The Mongols believed that the souls of just men fly from the mountain peaks to heaven.

Battlement Ornament (fig. 12) is found mainly on woven carpets, where it is the natural result of the technique.

The **Hourglass** (fig. 13) is a symbol of eternity; found on Caucasian carpets.

A geometrical design known as a **Galley** border (fig. 14) – because it resembles men rowing – mainly appears in Caucasian carpets made in the coastal areas of the Black Sea.

The swastika in a complex form became the **Hook** design (fig. 15), found mainly in the Caucasus, Turkestan and on some Persian carpets.

7

8

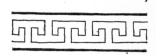

9

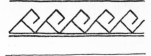
11

13

12

10

14

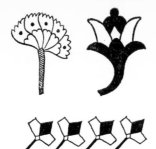

20   21   22   23

15

The **Wineglass** (fig. 16) – the Caucasus, Armenia.

The **Herringbone** (fig. 17), the symbol of wealth and health – the Caucasus, in Turkestan.

Turkoman Line (fig. 18), a broken line – Turkestan.

The **Candlestick** (fig. 19).

Flowers

16

Flowers, buds and blossom standing for the vegetation of Paradise are frequently used. Occasionally, in some of the very old luxury carpets of India, the whole plant, with roots and flowers appears. Bunches of flowers were given the shape of palms, derived from the Egyptian palmette, which holds symbolical meaning.

17

The **Carnation** (fig. 20) – prayer carpets from Asia Minor and Morocco.

The **Tulip** (fig. 21) – Asia Minor.

The **Lotus** was the sacred flower of Buddha, the symbol of immortality and purity.

The **Lily** (fig. 22) in Persia and India is the symbol of virginity, purity.

Rhodes Lily – Konya, Asia Minor.

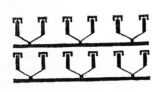

18

19

The tongue shape of the **Iris** (fig. 23) gave it the position of interpreter of flowers; it was also a symbol of religious freedom and the liberator from earthly ties. Irises appear on luxury Indian and nomad carpets and carpets from Persia and Kurdistan.

The **Pomegranate** (fig. 24), which decorated the robes of Assyrian and Jewish priests, represented fertility. It is very occasionally found on carpets from Asia Minor or Persia.

The **Chrysanthemum**, used mainly in China, is the symbol of happiness and fertility.

In Persia divine power was ascribed to the **Rose (Rosette)** (fig. 25). It was the symbol of eternal life as well and occurs on carpets from Chinese Turkestan.

24   25   26

27

The flower of the **Henna** (an Egyptian privet), the favourite flower of Mohammed, occurs in Persia.

Leaves

Leaves are found chiefly on luxury carpets; they hardly ever appear in the work of nomads. Leaves are one of the few features which help to determine age. They appear in a large variety of different designs, but there are three basic types which are:

General Leaf Shapes (fig. 26) with two or three indentations; in a highly stylised form (often like clover leaves) they are typical in ancient Armenian Joraghany carpets.

28

Lanceolate Leaves (fig. 27), spearhead shapes tapering to each end, which were originally derived from the wild acanthus. Sometimes they are fish-shaped; the fish was the sacred symbol of the goddess Isis. Found often on old Persian carpets of 1500 to 1700 and after 1630 in increasing sizes; in Asia Minor they have rich, so-called Syrian forms.

29

Saracenic Trefoils (fig. 28), derived from Saracenic art, appear often in borders on old Persian carpets.

The many complex variations of **Tendril** and **Stem** patterns (fig. 29) (spirals, arabesques, waves and criss-crosses), adapted from antique models, are most often found on luxury carpets from Persia and Asia Minor and hardly ever on nomad work. Highly stylised floral **Stems** are typical of Ushak and Transylvanian carpets. On Persian luxury carpets the **Tendrils** often formed the border. Endless **Intertwined Tendrils** were the symbol of endurance, repetition.

Trees

Trees had many associations and many primitive nations believed that the souls of just men rose with the branches of tall trees and the peaks of mountains to heaven.

The Persians had two kinds of sacred trees: *Allsamen* and *Allheil*. The seeds of the tree fell to the ground the moment the mystical eagle alighted upon it. Under its weight a thousand branches broke and the seeds were scattered. When the bird rose on the wing, the branches straightened out again. The

30

33

31

32

33

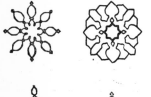

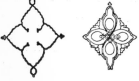

Haoma tree was the Paradise tree of life. Whoever tasted its juice would be immortal.

The Indians combined the qualities of both trees to make the *Soma*, the symbol of immortality. Each country has a particular tree sacred to it: in antique art it is the fig tree and the vine; in eastern Turkestan, the cedar; in Persia, the cypress. The trees on nomad carpets from western Turkestan resemble fir trees with cones.

The development of the depiction of the tree on Persian carpets is an aid in dating them; around 1400 to 1470 the drawing of the tree was crude and archaic; branches had fruit but no leaves. In the period 1470 to 1600 leaves were added; before then trees and bushes are depicted with roots and soil. After 1600 flowers appeared on both Persian and Indian carpets. In India and Persia groups of tree carpets were made.

Weeping Willow trees (fig. 30), the symbol of death, are usually found on funerary carpets, with which the dead were covered.

The **Palm,** which appears in Persian carpets, was the symbol of the fulfilment of secret wishes.

The **Coconut Palm** provides the Indians with many of the necessities of life: timber, oil, medicines, food, fibre for clothing and rugs, hence it is the tree of requests and the fulfilment of wishes.

The **Cypress** (fig. 31), the symbol of sorrow and, because of its permanently green leaves, symbol of the future, is often found on tomb or funerary carpets and on ancient Persian Kerman and Shiraz carpets.

The **Tree of Life** (fig. 32) originates in ancient Assyria.

Medallions (fig. 33)

The central motif of the inner field is often formed by a medallion. There are numerous different shapes: spiral scrolls, diamonds, clover leaves, flames,

33

34

arabesques, trefoils, circles (the old Chinese symbol of natural strength), *yin-yang* (circular medallion divided by a wavy line into two shapes of fishes, the darker part *yin* – the female symbol, the strength of birth, the lighter part *yang* – the male strength of fertility), the *Shu* medallion (originally a circular geometrical written character, in seventeenth-century China used with a dragon motif, later with leaves and blossom), pole-shapes (mostly three to five medallions joined with bars), the *Turunji* medallion (four forked tendrils found in Persia).

The most complex and richest forms are on Persian and Indian carpets. On some old Persian carpets of 1500 to 1680 the central medallion is in the shape of a cartouche formed like a cross or coat of arms. Transylvanian carpets from Asia Minor have geometrical cartouches along the border.

The origins of **Palmette** designs (fig. 34) lie in the lotus flower or the fruit of the pomegranate. The different types are named according to their shape and content: wreath-shaped – surrounded by a wreath;
chalice – with the central motif of a chalice;
fan – where the outer contours resemble an open fan;
leaf-shaped – made up of motifs of leaves;
Byzantine or Saracenic – made of folded scroll-shaped leaves. (This appeared in early Muslim art at the time Byzantine motifs of ornamentation were still in use);
arabesque – composed of arabesque loops;
Shah Abbas – the most widespread, had an isolated motif in the centre, separated by a single line, on a single coloured background.

35

The **Arabesque** (fig. 35), a flat ornament, composed of circular or spiral tendrils, existed wherever religious principles prohibited the depiction of human beings and animals: Egypt, north Africa, Turkey, India, in some areas of Persia, and in Spain.

Herati (fig. 36), a very varied, floral, diamond-shaped motif with four projecting leaves, is found on all Persian carpets (particularly Feraghan, Khorasan and Sehna).

36

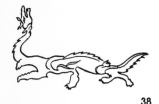

37

38

Animals

Nomad carpets often have stylised household animals such as dogs, cocks, camels. On Persian luxury carpets highly naturalistic wild animals are depicted, usually in hunting scenes.

Mythical Animals

The **Dragon** (fig. 37) was a very popular mythical animal in all countries. It is frequent on Persian carpets where there was a cult of the demon dragon; in China it is a symbol of infinity and Imperial power, in India a symbol of death.

The **She-dragon** (fig. 38), depicted as a winged serpent and with a body of a crocodile, is found on some old Indian luxury carpets.

39

The legendary **Phoenix** (fig. 39), which rose alive out of ashes, is a symbol of life and immortality; appears either in pairs or individually on old Persian and old Indian luxury carpets.

40

The **Ch'i-lin** (fig. 40), an animal with the body of a stag, a bull's tail and one horn on its head, is a sacred animal in China, and found on Chinese carpets.

41   42

Other Animals

Foxes, stags, lynxes, hares, wolves, jackals, panthers, tigers, lions, leopards, goats, antelopes, gazelles, elephants and deer, each of which bear a symbolical significance in different countries, appear on Chinese and Indian luxury carpets. They are often depicted as part of hunting scenes.

Camels (fig. 41) and **Pigs** – on nomad carpets.

43

Dogs (fig. 42) on nomad carpets are shown highly stylised; on Persian carpets they always wear a collar as symbol of loyalty. A dog without a collar meant a lowly state.

The **Eagle** appears in all types of Oriental decoration on fabrics and architecture as well as carpets, but often stylised beyond recognition. They appear most frequently on old luxury carpets and on nomad carpets from western Turkestan.

44   45

46

Among the **Birds,** parrots (fig. 43), hawks, storks, herons, peacocks, partridges, geese and ducks are all found on luxury carpets from India and Persia, bearing a variety of symbolic meanings. Storks, peacocks and herons are frequent on Chinese carpets; cocks are confined to Persian and nomad works.

47

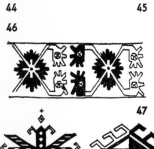

Fish (fig. 44) in many variations are often found in borders or framing other motifs, sometimes they cover the entire area. Fish are particularly common to Chinese, Persian-Armenian, Persian Herat, Sehna, Feraghan, Khorasan carpets.

22

48

The **Serpent** (fig. 45), as a symbol of knowledge and wisdom, appears on old Indian carpets.

The **Butterfly,** the symbol of flirtation, is found in China and India.

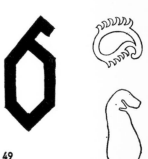

49

Tortoises, one of India's four divine animals, are portrayed realistically on Indian luxury carpets. In China they are a symbol of a long life. Highly stylised tortoises occur on nomad carpets, particularly in borders.

Crabs (fig. 46) are found on the borders of Caucasian carpets.

Spiders, Scorpions, Tarantulas (fig. 47) are woven into carpets as protection against their highly painful bites. On Caucasian nomad carpets from western and eastern Turkestan they are often a theme in borders.

50

Fighting Animals, typical in old Oriental carpets, are the religious symbols of the struggle of good and evil, the triumph of good over evil, night over day, and the stronger over the weaker. Most of the animals shown are wild: lions, tigers, panthers about to overcome stags, antelopes, bulls.

Fighting Dragons, found on Chinese and later Persian carpets, belong to the store of Chinese symbolism, from where they later passed into Mongolian myths.

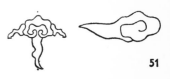

51

Human Figures

Human figures are only strictly banned by some Islamic sects. Thus humans do appear on certain Persian carpets, particularly as motifs of decorative importance within larger compositions, on luxury carpets showing hunting scenes. Stylised, simplified human figures also occur on nomad carpets (fig. 48).

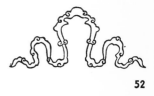

52

Miscellaneous

53

Mina-khani is a pair of flowers repeated against a lattice, or a large central flower surrounded by four small ones.

The **Mir-i-bota** motif (fig. 49) resembles the print of a closed fist or finger; it is thought to have originated from the mark of fist or finger dipped in blood, with which rulers identified their possessions. These patterns are sometimes thought to be flames, fir cones, the meandering bed of the river Indus or Ganges or another river. They are used in Persia and India in the inner field, often covering the entire area.

54

55

Chintamani (fig. 50), three balls, spheres or pearls, is the emblem both of the Buddha and of the Mongolian conqueror, Timur, who in 1402 subdued the Turks in Asia Minor.

Chi (fig. 51), the symbol of immortality, a cloud in various shapes: curved, massive, shell-like, like a ribbon, surrounded by clouds and lightning, occurs in Persia, China and the Caucasus.

Cloud-band (fig. 52), derived from the Chi motif, which it shows in a stylised group. Between 1500 and 1680 it was an important motif in Persian art and on Persian carpets from the period of the Saphids.

Lightning (fig. 53), two twisted stripes symbolising clouds, wool, lightning or fire, is found on all types of Oriental carpets.

Sacrificial Stick (fig. 54) – western Turkestan.

56

Knot of Fate (fig. 55), the infinite symbol of the Buddha, occurs in China, Caucasus, Samarkand.

Lamps, Vases, Jugs, Compasses (fig. 56), **Combs** (fig. 57) are woven into prayer rugs as objects essential for offering prayers. Combs also refer to the combs used in weaving to tighten the weft threads and knots.

57

Inscriptions

Inscriptions on carpets mostly have a decorative and ornamental significance and are often illegible. On older carpets quotations from Arab poets, the names of rulers or the date sometimes appear. But they are little help in dating because, as with other motifs, they are often repeated on more modern carpets. Inscriptions are found most frequently on Persian luxury carpets of 1500 to 1650.

Chinese Script Signs of Happiness (fig. 58).

Kufic Script (fig. 59), the oldest form of Islamic writing, is often found on Oriental carpets. The name is derived from the town of Kufa in Mesopotamia.

58

Thurga Inscription (fig. 60), the signature of Sultan Abdul-Aziz, is supposed to have been written in blood with three fingers of the right hand. Its stylised form appears more often on embroideries than on carpets.

Arabic Script (fig. 61).

North-African Script (fig. 62).

59

61

62

60

63

Turkish Script (fig. 63).

Egyptian Script (fig. 64).

Arabic Numerals (fig. 65).

Chinese Symbols

The Eight Taoist Symbols (fig. 66).

The Eight Buddhist Symbols (fig. 67).

The Symbols of the Arts (fig. 68).

66

The Symbolism of Colours

All ancient cultures, and particularly that of China, endowed symbolic meaning to colours. The land (yellow) was conquered from the forest (green) and sends to the surface metal (white), which then overpowered the wood, but has first to soften the glare of fire (red). Water (black) finally becomes victor in the struggle with fire.

67

Green is the sacred colour of the Muslims; it is the colour of the Prophet, of his battle banner, which he bore aloft in the fight against the unbelievers, and of the turban, worn by those who visit Mecca as pilgrims. As it is a sacred colour, it is used only rarely on carpets, and then only for small motifs, never as a large patch of colour.

The background and borders are often **Blue** which, for the Persians, was a symbol of the sky, of eternity, and for the Mongolians indicated strength.

Red is very often the basic colour of the carpet, a symbol of happiness, joy, wealth.

Yellow is a symbol of piety, and hence the colour of the robes of dervishes.

In the Orient **White** is the colour of sorrow.

68

The survey that follows includes the most important and well-known types of carpets. The categories into which they can be placed are largely based on commercial practice, as this, unfortunately, is the only system that has been clearly established. The names of new carpets are often almost accidentally chosen according to their place of origin, the town where they are sold, a certain trade centre, or a tribe. Today when in all areas almost every kind of carpet is made, and when the particular features of design and craftsmanship of individual regions have disappeared, these labels are somewhat inadequate. As yet no new nomenclature has been compiled, so, for the sake of categorisation, this system, with all its shortcomings, has to be used.

Art historians still lack sufficient knowledge of dating, provenance and the development of design to be able to work out a new system based not on place of production, but on evolutionary trends.

IRAN

Persia (now called Iran) has always excelled in the making of carpets and may well be the country in which they first came into existence. Their repertoire of gently curving flowers, animals and patterns is the richest in the entire Orient. The numerous centres of production, scattered throughout the country, provide a wealth of different varieties. Persian carpets were made both by nomads and, particularly the ancient luxury carpets, in Imperial factories. Both types are technically excellent and made of good quality materials.

Antique Carpets (Chronology is here relative)

Archaic, luxury carpets, c. 1250—1400. These were probably first made under the Mongol dynasties and under the Timurids.
Colours: ivory, deep brick red, blue; borders often black or dark blue.
Design: archaic pattern, narrow border.

Carpets with large medallions, c. 1400—1490.
Colouus: ivory is predominant, with brick red, and dark blue border.
Design: a large star-shaped medallion fills up almost the entire area of the inner field. The connecting tendrils are only rarely covered with leaves or flowers. Some examples have already broader borders.

Carpets with small medallions, c. 1480—1550.
Colours: white is predominant, reds and purples, with black border.
Design: the centre of the pattern is formed by a small medallion in the shape of a lemon surrounded by tendrils and leaves with buds and palmettes. The border is broad and often covered with stylized arabesques.

Shah Abbas, c. 1550—1630.
Design: tendrils with flowers and buds, with *chi* and cloud-band motifs, which were introduced to Persia in about 1600, mainly through the Chinese craftsmen of the Ming emperors, who were brought to the court of Shah Abbas.

Floral, c. 1650—1720.
Design: these are already divided in the classical way with a medallion in the central field and corners, filled with flowers entwined with spiral tendrils and large palmette flowers.

Isfahan, c. 1650—1700.

Design: the entire area of the carpet is covered with a network of tendrils. They get their name from the capital of Shah Abbas I.

The categories above are chronological divisions. Carpets can also be divided according to the nature of their design, irrespective of period, on the basis of the few examples that have survived.

'Polonais' carpets. Made mainly in the middle of the seventeenth century. These carpets were given as presents to Polish monarchs. The carpets look as if they were produced very quickly; their fabric is loose and they have a high pile.
Materials: sometimes gold or silver threads were used, or silk.
Knots: Sehna.
Size: 1.40 × 2.20 m.
Colours: bright brick orange, green, blue; some carpets have no red whatever and use only a cold blue shade with the smaller areas in yellow and green, sometimes brown.
Design: a central field in the shape of a star with corners, and the rest of the area filled with tendrils. The borders tend to have balanced Saracenic trefoils, flowers or arabesques, elsewhere a reciprocal line pattern.
   The name 'Polonais' dates from the Paris World Exhibition of 1878, when Count Czartoryski exhibited a large quantity of such carpets, several of which bore the coat of arms of his family. The letter M, which is woven into the borders of certain pieces, led to the false attribution to the Polish Mazarski factory at Sluck. The origin of the carpets is, however, far older than the existence of this factory and the entire technique and pattern in any case points to an undeniable Persian origin. They may have been produced in the court factories at Yezd or Kashan. They must have been made as gifts as none have been found in Persia. A 'Polonais' carpet appears as a table covering in a picture by G. Pencz of 1534 (*Male Portrait*, Berlin), which thus may serve as a *terminus ante quem*. Later there are several recorded presents, for instance to Pope Urban VII, to the Roman families of Colonna and Corsini, and in 1604 to the Doge of Venice.

Hunting carpets. These are very precious and only very few examples have survived. Their designs of fights between animals, hunters and flowers show that they were based on Assyrian-Babylonian art. The animals portrayed include: Chinese phoenix, dragons, *ch'i-lin*, lions, tigers, panthers, leopards, bears, stags, gazelles, antelopes, dogs, jackals, wild boars, foxes, hares, monkeys, serpents, tortoises, peacocks, parrots, partridges, eagles, geese, ducks and other birds.
   One very valuable example, now in the Kunsthistorisches Museum, Vienna, was a gift from Tsar Peter the Great to Emperor Leopold I.

Animal carpets, fifteenth to seventeenth centuries. The designs use the classical layout with a star-shaped medallion in the centre, and sometimes others along the longer sides and in the corners. Other motifs include: cloudbands, *chi*, *ch'i-lin*, phoenix, dragons, *chintamani*, bats and lightning. The carpets must have been made under the Safavid dynasty in the factories at Herat, Tabriz and Isfahan.

'Portuguese' carpets, seventeenth century. Classical layout with a central diamond-shaped medallion surrounded by frets, with floral motifs, boats with Europeans and animals. Only a small group of carpets has survived, clearly made for export to Portugal or Goa.

Garden carpets. Such as the garden carpet of Chosroes I described on p. 8.

Between 1650 and 1750 several series of garden carpets, made of wool and silk, were made in western Persia. Their usual size was 2.30 × 3 m. to 2.20 × 5 m.

Carpets with lanceolate leaves, 1600—1750. These have no central design, but a main motif of large lanceolate leaves. Some older pieces are very precious.

Carpets with forked tendrils, c. 1550—1750. These resemble the previous group, the main motif being forked tendrils.

Carpets with diamond patterns. The design is based on an old scheme, frequently found on nomad carpets to this day, of subdividing the entire area into diamond-shaped fields. At the time of the Safavid dynasty they were made in the town of Kerman.

Cartouche carpets, c. 1580—1700. These have the classical layout of an inner field with a central cartouche medallion, which is repeated in the border.

Herat carpets, end of the sixteenth to early eighteenth centuries. These very dense carpets take their name from the town where they were made. They were clearly intended for export and many were found in Europe and in mosques in India and Turkey. They do not appear in Italian paintings, but are frequently depicted by Flemish artists, for instance, in Rubens' series of the life of Maria de Medici.
Materials: wool and occasionally silk.
Knots: 40 to 1 sq.cm.
Sizes: older carpets: 2.50 × 4 m. or 8 × 15 m., after 1680 they were smaller: 1.20 × 2.50 m., and 1.80 × 3.50 m.
Colours: background: black or ivory; pattern: red, green, blue and yellow.
Design: the area of the carpet is densely covered with a regular Herati pattern which later appears on all types of Persian carpets.

Tree carpets, 1400—1550. Symmetrical patterns of trees (cypresses, trees with flowers, fruits and palmettes) cover the area of the carpet. The broad borders are decorated with arabesques. The trees on carpets from the earliest phase, 1400 to 1480, do not have leaves.

Joshaghan carpets, 1500—1850. The predominant feature of the design is a palmette, peculiar to Joshaghan, where these dense, firmly woven carpets were made. Arab records state that in about 1550 they were exported to India. Production came to an end when the town was destroyed.

Carpets with bunches of flowers. The inner field is filled with naturalistically designed bunches of flowers, particularly roses, drawn as seen from above. The main colours are red, blue and brown. Today the motif of the *gül* rose appears on almost all Persian and Caucasian carpets. They were made in the town of Kashan in the province of Irak-i-Ajam; more recently similar carpets with smaller flowers were made at Kerman.

Vase carpets, 1500—1680. They came into existence at the time of the Safavids, probably in southern Persia, possibly in the town of Kerman, and used to be discovered in Italian churches and Oriental bazaars.
Sizes: long and narrow, usually 2.2 × 5 m.
Colours: mainly ivory, sometimes red-brown, purplish-red.
Design: the main motif is a vase with a network of tendrils with blossom, palmettes and the *chi* motif.

Coronation carpets. A coronation carpet, now in Castle Rosenborg, Copenhagen, which was presented by the Dutch East India Company to King Frederick III of Denmark in 1666, is used to this day during the coronation ceremony. **Size:** 3.10 × 5.28 m.

The Ardebil carpet. The Victoria and Albert Museum, London, possesses this carpet (10.34 × 5.20 m.) which was made for the large mosque at Ardebil in northern Persia and was probably produced at Kashan. It bears the inscription: 'I have no refuge in the world other than thy threshold, my head has no protection other than this porchway. The work of the slave of this Holy Place. Maksud of Kasham in the year 946' (1540).

An English carpet firm acquired it from the mosque in the 1880's and in 1893 the Museum bought it for £ 2,000.

Semi-Antique and Modern Persian Carpets

Abadeh. From the town of Abadeh in southern Iran on the road from Shiraz to Isfahan.
Materials: wool and cotton.
Knots: Sehna.
Colours: red, terracotta, brown, blue, a little green.
Design: a central field with a diamond-shaped medallion or one in the shape of a clover-leaf, the rest of the area is filled in with small stylised flowers or leaves.

Afshar. (Sometimes known, in the trade, as Saidabad or Sirdshan.) Producers nomads or semi-nomads in the area between Shiraz and Kerman. They are the inhabitants that originally lived between the Tigris and the Euphrates and who under the rule of Shah Abbas migrated to Persia.
Materials: cotton, wool.
Knots: Ghiordes, occasionally Sehna; density per sq.cm.: 7—15.
Size: 1.20 × 1.80 m.
Colours: bright, on a red or blue background, often white or cream-coloured and other pastel shades.
Design: central field is filled with a diamond pattern with stylised flowers, stiff tendrils, barber's poles, rosettes, *mir-i-bota*, motifs reminiscent of Caucasian ones.

Ardebil (plate 8). From the neighbourhood of the town of Ardebil (today Ardabil) in northern Iran.
Materials: wool and cotton.
Knots: Ghiordes, density per sq.cm.: 12—18.
Size: 2 × 3 m.
Basic colours: red, blue and cream.
Design: highly stylised, with a medallion in the centre and a square with flowers, like the Caucasian Shirvan.

Bakhtiari. The producers are nomad tribes in southern Iran between Isfahan and the Persian Gulf, who came originally from Turkey.
Materials: cotton and wool.
Knots: Ghiordes, density per sq.cm.: 6—20.
Sizes: 1.20 × 1.80 m., 5.00 × 3.50 m., and square.
Colours: predominantly red, brown, blue and cream.
Design: the central field is normally divided into smaller fields, frequently square, with flowers, rosettes or squares; the motif of the tree of life is frequent. Each tribe had its own characteristic features.

Bijar (plate 18). The producers of these numerous old carpets are Kurds, no-mads and semi-nomads, and factories in the province of Ardilan in northern Iran.
Materials: cotton, wool or camel hair.
Knots: Ghiordes or Sehna, density per sq.cm.: 7—20.
Sizes: 1.50×2.40 m., 2.20×3 m., 2.50×3.50 m., 1×4.50 m., 6×4 m.
Colours: red, blue, yellow, ivory, the natural shade of camel hair, black, dark blue.
Design: the central field is filled with an arabesque and corner sectors, some-times with small vase motifs, stylised flowers, trees, birds, animals and human figures. The border often has Herati motifs, rosettes and tendrils.

Feraghan (plates 7, 10, 29, 33). From the district of Feraghan in central Iran, east of Hamadan. Between 1880 and 1914 these carpets were produced for the European and American markets.
Materials: cotton, camel hair, wool.
Knots: Sehna, density per sq.cm.: 7—20.
Sizes: 2 × 3 m., up to 6 × 10 m., 2.40 × 2 m., 7 × 3.50 m.
Colours: dark, quiet – beige, blue, red – using all the customary tones of Oriental carpets.
Design: originally had the typical Herati pattern, but, during the period when Feraghan carpets were made for export, they imitated ancient luxury carpets with large medallions and corners. The carpet can be recognised by the strong cotton warp which is clearly visible on the back. The border has rosettes, flowers, leaves, arabesques and tendrils.

Ghoum. From the town of Ghoum (today Qum) south of Teheran, in one of the oldest towns of the country.
Materials: wool; warp – cotton.
Knots: Sehna, density per sq.cm.: 15—60.
Sizes: all current sizes and runners 1.50 × 6.00 m.
Basic colours: cream, dark and light blue, less often red, often multi-coloured patterns.
Design: a central medallion, using the flame motif, vases, also motifs placed in straight or diagonal rows. The border has floral motifs, Shah Abbas and arrow-points.

Hamadan (plates 2, 5). From some two thousand villages surrounding the town of Hamadan in central Persia.
Materials: warp – cotton; weft – wool or, except in the more recent carpets, camel hair.
Knots: Ghiordes, density per sq.cm.: 5—12.
Sizes: 2.50 × 3.50 m., 5.50 × 5 m., 4 × 6 m., small ones: 1.10 × 1.40 m.
Colours: blue, red, less often green, the natural colours of camel hair, the borders include yellow.
Design: motifs are varied, often with a medallion in the centre, human or ani-mal motifs primitively stylised. The composition of the inner field is divided into a central medallion and corners.

Herat. From eastern Iran, now Afghanistan.
Materials: warp – cotton; weft – wool.
Knots: Ghiordes, density per sq.cm.: 18—25.
Sizes: 2.50 × 3,50 m., 4 × 6 m.
Colours: red is predominant and dark blue.
Design: includes the Herati motif in the field and border, less frequently the *mir-i-bota*, in regular layout. The border has rosettes and lotus flowers.

Herez. Produced, particularly between 1880 and 1900, in the town of Herez east of Tabriz in central Iran, and in the smaller towns of Serapi, Gorevan, Bakhshis.

Materials: warp – cotton; weft – cotton or wool.
Knots: Ghiordes, density per sq.cm.: 4—14.
Sizes: 3 × 4 m., 3.50 × 5 m., 4 × 5.50 m., sometimes as much as 7 m. long and even 8 × 5 m.
Colours: light blue, green, dark terracotta, light yellow, on a red background.
Design: archaic motifs, geometrical patterns, arabesques, stylised flowers, star-shaped medallion. Narrow border with the Herati motif, triangles and rosettes.

Isfahan (plate 12). The production of carpets following classical patterns still continues in Isfahan where Shah Abbas set up a workshop.
Materials: warp – cotton; weft – wool.
Knots: Sehna, density per sq.cm.: 20 – 50.
Sizes: mainly runners, 1.20 × 2.00 m., 2.50 × 3.80 m.
Basic colours: red, beige, light blue, with multi-coloured patterns.
Design: basic motif is twisted tendrils, with or without a medallion, lotus flowers, animal motifs, inscriptions; the border, which is sometimes joined to the inner field, contains the Shah Abbas motif.

Joshaghan (plate 16). Production mainly in the eighteenth and early nineteenth centuries, in central Iran, north of Isfahan.
Materials: warp – cotton; weft – cotton or wool.
Knots: Sehna, density per sq.cm.: 8—15.
Sizes: runners and large pieces up to 7 m. long.
Colours: bright, mainly blue, with red and beige.
Design: Tabriz and Kashan motifs with small squares enclosing stylised flowers or tendrils. Sometimes with a large diamond-shaped medallion in the centre. Flower motifs along the border.

Kashan (plates 8, 22, 39). The town of Kashan between Teheran and Isfahan has a long tradition of carpet-making which was interrupted for several hundred years.
These carpets are used as wall-hangings in Persia.
Materials: warp – cotton; weft – cotton or wool; pile – wool or silk.
Knots: Ghiordes and Sehna, density per sq.cm.: 30—50 in wool, 40—80 in silk.
Sizes: 2 × 3 m., 2.50 × 3.50 m.. 3 × 4 m., 3.50 × 4.50 m.
Colours: multi-coloured patterns, with red, blue or ivory as basic colours.
Design: inner field has a central medallion and corners with designs of lotus flowers, columns, the Herati motif and vases.

Kashgai (plate 34). They are produced mainly by the women of the Kashgai, one of the largest nomad tribes living over a wide territory to the north-west of Shiraz.
Materials: wool with mixture of animal hair.
Knots: Sehna and sometimes Ghiordes.
Basic colours: red, reddish-brown, blue, cream.
Design: small geometrical motifs: rosettes, stars, crosses, leaves, birds and diamonds.

Kenedagh. Produced in the district of Karadagh in north-western Azerbaijan, they flooded European markets between 1890 and 1910.
Materials: wool, camel and goat hair.
Knots: Ghiordes and Sehna.
Sizes: runners of 0.80 × 1.10 m. and 0.90 × 1.40 m.

These are rough carpets of dull, uncleaned material; the patterns are very similar to Caucasian. Nomad Kenedagh carpets of better quality also exist.

Nomad Kenedagh.
Materials: good wool and cotton.
Knots: Ghiordes and Sehna.
Sizes: 1.10 × 1.60 m., 1.40 × 2 m., 2 × 4 m.
Colours: the ground is purple, grass green, white, the border red.
Design: they often used Herati motifs.

Kerman (plate 38). The town of Kerman in the province of the same name has an old tradition of carpet-making. Carpets from the neighbouring towns of Yezd and Rawar are sometimes labelled as Yezd-Kerman and Rawar-Kerman.
Materials: warp – cotton; weft – cotton, wool; pile – wool.
Knots: Sehna, density per sq.cm.: 25—40.
Sizes: 1.20 × 1.90 m., 2 × 3 m., 3 × 4 m., 3.50 × 5 m., 0.70 × 1.70 m.
Basic colours: pastel shades, light cream, green, blue, dark red, with brightly coloured design.
Design: central medallion with corners on the inner field, rich floral ornaments with tendrils, rosettes, conventionalised roses, sometimes palmettes are repeated on the ground. The nineteenth-century carpets have animal and floral designs. Carpets which were adapted to European taste bear the influence of French Baroque ornaments. The border has floral stems, trees of life, lotus flowers, palmettes, meanders and rosettes.

Kermanshah. Production in the town of Kermanshah, the main town of the south-west of Hamadan.
Materials: wool and cotton.
Knots: Sehna and Ghiordes, density per sq.cm.: 12—20.
Sizes: 2.50 × 3.50 m., 3 × 4 m., 4 × 6 m.
Colours: very harmonious with no single colour predominating; light tones with a blue, red and ivory ground.
Design: basic composition is formed by a dense network of tendrils with blossom and foliage; sometimes there is a large central design of Herati, arabesques, and *mir-i-bota* motifs.

Khorasan (plates 9, 11, 13, 27). From the province of Khorasan.
Materials: cotton and wool.
Knots: Sehna, density per sq.cm.: 6—25.
Sizes: 0.90 × 1.50 m., 1.20 × 1.80 m., 2 × 3.50 m., 2.50 × 5 m.
Colours: red, central field, often with bluish-pink colouring, elsewhere dark blue with green shading.
Design: there are three groups of modern production:
1900—1914 carpets produced in the town of Kaiz of rather poor quality, loosely woven, irregularly knotted.
1900—1914 better quality carpets that originated under European influence, produced in the town of Birdshan.
1800—1880 the best quality carpets. The inner field has a central design with corners, naturalistic birds and animal patterns, and a broad border.

Luristan. Producers were the Bakhtiari nomads in the inaccessible parts of western Iran.
Materials: warp – cotton; weft and pile – wool with animal hair.
Knots: Ghiordes, density per sq.cm.: 6—10.
Sizes: 0.90 × 1.60 m., rugs as much as 3.80 m. long, 1.50 × 4 m.
Basic colours: dark blue, red and ivory, with brightly coloured patterns.

Design: large flowers, rows of rosettes, borders with twisted tendrils, crabs, rosettes, stars, one to three medallions, flowers, star-shaped designs.

Mahal. Also known as Muskabad they are produced in central Iran in the neighbourhood of Feraghan.
Materials: warp – cotton; weft – cotton; pile – wool.
Knots: Ghiordes, density per sq.cm.: 4—8.
Sizes: rugs and carpets – 6 m. long, 4.50 × 6 m.
Basic colours: red, blue, beige.
Design: often has Herati patterns in the main field and along the border; there is sometimes a medallion on the smooth ground. Shah Abbas rosettes, flowers, *mir-i-bota*, Herati.

Meshed. The town of Meshed in the province of Khorasan was the centre for carpets woven by nomad craftsmen of the entire neighbourhood.
Materials: warp – cotton; weft – wool; pile – wool.
Knots: Sehna, density per sq.cm.: 10—18.
Sizes: 2.50 × 3.50 m., to 6 × 8 m.
Basic colours: blue, red, light pink, cream-coloured pattern.
Design: the inner field is divided into a central medallion and corner sections, with rich floral ornaments, and a broad border with up to twelve guard stripes in the Herati design.

Mir. Produced in central Iran, in the area of Feraghan.
Materials: warp – cotton; weft – wool or goat hair; pile – wool.
Knots: density per sq.cm.: 15—30.
Sizes: runners up to 1.80 m. long, 1.50—2.50 × 4.50 m.
Basic colours: blue, red and beige, with up to twelve colours in the pattern.
Design: the inner field has Seraband palmettes, the border conventionalised lotus flowers, arabesques, foliage, flowers, rosettes and arrow-points.

Mosul. Produced in the neighbourhood of the town of Hamadan. The name is after the market centre where they are sold.
Materials: wool, camel and goat hair, cotton.
Knots: Ghiordes, density per sq.cm.: 4—6.
Size: 1.30 × 2 m.
Colours: red, blue, green, brown, which differ from carpet to carpet, as does the quality.
Design: patterns from Seraband and Herati carpets.

Muskabad. Produced in central Iran, in the area of Feraghan.
Materials: warp – cotton; weft – wool or goat hair; pile – wool.
Knots: Sehna, density per sq.cm.: 8—12.
Size: 1.30 × 2.20 m.
Basic colours: red and blue.
Design: large with conventionalised flowers in rows, and stylised arabesques. The border has flowers and broken arabesques, hour-glass patterns and S-borders.

Saruk (plates 4, 14, 19, 30). Produced in the village of Saruk, south-west of Teheran.
Materials: wool and cotton.
Knots: Sehna, density per sq.cm.: 20—40.
Sizes of runners and long carpets: 2.20 × 5 m., 1.20 × 1.80 m., 4 × 6 m.
Basic colours: blue, red, sometimes beige.
Design: reminiscent of the Kerman or Kashan carpets, is sometimes divided

into a central medallion and corner sections with tendrils. At other times, several medallions are scattered over the carpets.

Sehna. Produced in the neighbourhood of the town of Sehna (today known as Sanandaj).
Materials: warp – cotton; weft – wool, cotton; pile – wool, silk.
Knots: Sehna, density per sq.cm.: 25—50.
Sizes: 1.20 × 1.80 m., largest size 2.40 m.
Basic colours: blue, red, sapphire green, pink, yellow, white.
Design: small patterns of flames, Herati, palmettes are scattered over the entire carpet. The border has tortoise and flower designs.

The design of *ch'i-lin* carpets from Sehna, which are blue, red with a little orange, brown and green, is a lozenge-shaped field with highly conventionalised tendrils, flowers and palmettes.

Seraband. Produced in the mountain area, in western Iraq-i-adshemi.
Materials: warp – cotton; weft – wool, cotton; pile – wool.
Knots: Ghiordes and Sehna, density per sq.cm.: 15—30.
Sizes: 2 × 3.50 m., 2.50 × 4 m., 3.40 × 5.20 m., small loosely woven carpets 1.50 m. long.
Basic colours: red, blue and ivory.
Design: the *mir-i-bota* motif, or a design of small tulips in rows alternately inclined to the right and to the left, are repeated all over in a regular design. The wide borders have three stripes with tendril and arabesque designs.

Shiraz (plate 17). Produced by the nomad Kashgai tribes, and after 1890, also by craftsmen in the town of Shiraz where they were gathered from all over the Farsistan province.
Materials: warp – wool, goat hair; weft – goat hair; pile – wool.
Knots: Sehna and Ghiordes, density per sq.cm.: 6—10.
Sizes: 0.70 × 1.20 m., 1.10 × 1.60 m., 1.50 × 2.90 m., 2 × 3 m., 2.50 × 3.50 m., 3 × 4 m., and larger.
Colours: sometimes sharply contrasting red and blue, less often cream.
Design: the lozenge-shaped field fills the entire centre of the carpet, often with stepped guard-stripes, tendrils, conventionalised animal and floral designs.

Tabriz (plate 3, 26, 28, 32, 35). Tabriz in the province of Azerbaijan is the centre of production and marketing for the entire neighbourhood (Herez, Sareb, Karadagh).
Materials: warp – wool, cotton and, in exceptional cases, silk.
Knots: Ghiordes, also Sehna, density per sq.cm.: 20—40.
Sizes: 2 × 3 m., 2.50 × 3.50 m., 3 × 4 m., 4 × 5 m., 8 × 12 m., and silk carpets: 1.20 × 1.80 m., 2 × 3 m., 2.50 × 3.50 m.
Colours: red or blue on a cream coloured ground.
Design: the inner field has a central medallion surrounded by smaller hunting designs and flower tendrils. The border of Herati motifs or lotus flowers with tendrils, often imitates the patterns of old luxury carpets.

Teheran (plates 15, 36). Factory production of the capital city of Teheran.
Materials: cotton and wool.
Knots: Sehna, density per sq.cm.: 20—40.
Sizes: up to 40 sq.m., 1.20 × 1.80 m., 1.40 × 2.50 m., 2 × 3 m., 3.00 × 4.50 m.
Colours: mainly blue, red and ivory on a light ground.
Designs: delicate floral patterns or medallions of various sizes.

Turkbaff. Produced in the province of Khorasan.

Materials: wool and cotton.
Knots: Ghiordes, density per sq.cm.: 8—15.
Sizes:: 2.50 × 3.50 m., 4 × 5 m.
Colours: light, almost, sweet, colour scheme; dark copper is typical.
Design: formed by a large medallion with corner sections; shows European influence.

Yezd. The town of Yezd, on the caravan route 200 km. east of Isfahan, was a market centre for carpets from a wide area.
Materials: wool and cotton.
Sizes: 0.80 × 1.30 m., 2.80 × 3.30 m., 3 × 4 m.
Colours: light, the whole carpet has a bluish-green tone, which is artificially achieved by washing.
Design: small geometrical and floral motifs.

CENTRAL ASIA

Carpets from this area come from western and eastern Turkestan, Afghanistan and Baluchistan. In all these areas the carpets are made mainly by nomads with a tradition of carpet production stretching far back into the past. Marco Polo already admired Turkoman carpets in the year 1280. The art flourished under the rule of the Timurids, who ruled Persia from 1369 to 1469, and Mongol patterns became incorporated into Persian art. In a similar way the Mongol emperors, who ruled India from 1526 to 1761 and were descended from Timur, influenced the spread of Persian characteristics in Indian design. Central Asian carpets were spared the commercial influences of Europe, as they were made in steppes and mountains remote from civilisation.

WESTERN TURKESTAN

The nomad carpet-making tribes were the Kirghiz of the northern steppes, the Kara-Kirghiz at Fergana and surroundings, the Kara-Kalpaks, who were once the mighty rulers of the Samarkand region, the Kisil Ayaks living near the Amu Darya river, not far from the borders of Afghanistan, and particularly the Turkomans who produced outstanding work, and are to this day famous for the beautiful carpets made in their territory. The character of all the carpets of the area is definitely nomadic. They are made of sheep's wool and goat and camel hair, and they are mostly densely tied in Sehna knots.

Today the carpets have been adapted in size to European dimensions; for, when the carpets were made entirely for local use, they were mainly small and for a particular purpose: bags for camels, saddle covers, door-hangings, floor carpets and wall-hangings. The Turkoman tent, *kibitka*, a circular construction on a wooden frame, is covered entirely with carpets and felt rugs. Double carpets, woven on one side and knotted inside, served as a kind of cupboard in the tents. The work was done mainly by women; girls made carpets for their bridegrooms to use as covers for their horses. A local saying maintains that the greater a man is loved, the more beautiful is the cover for his horse.

Beshir (plates 40, 45). The work of nomads of the Amu Darya river area near the town of Beshir (about 200 km. from Bokhara).
Materials: warp – wool, cotton or jute; weft – wool or goat hair; pile – wool.
Knots: Sehna, density per sq.cm.: 8—18.
Sizes: 4 × 3 m., 2 × 5 m., prayer rugs and bags are smaller.
Colours: mainly red and yellow, less frequently blue and green.
Design: small, geometrical stars, diamonds, S-shaped patterns, cloud-bands, rosettes, foliage; the central field is subdivided into several smaller fields.

Bokhara (plate 41). The carpets called by this name are made by the Tekke-

Turkoman nomadic tribes. Bokhara is the market centre where they are sold.
Materials: warp – jute; weft – wool; pile – wool, sometimes silk.
Knots: Sehna, density per sq.cm.: 25—45.
Size: runners and carpets 3.40 m. long.
Colours: various shades of red, the most beautiful carpets are of a shade of bull's blood, white and brown.
Design: inner field is made up of a row of octagons, with stars and octagons in the border.

Fergana. This region borders on Samarkand, Bokhara and eastern Turkestan. The producers were the Kara-Kirghiz and Kara-Kalpak tribes.
Material: wool.
Knots: Sehna, density per sq.cm.: 8—10.
Colours: dark chestnut red is predominant, and brick red on more modern carpets.
Design: a mixture of Turkoman and Beluchistan motifs very roughly executed.

Khiva. Made in what was formerly the *khanate* of Khiva, which in about 1190 was the centre of the powerful Khoras tribe. Work of the nomad Kara-Kirghiz, Kara-Kalpak and Yomud tribes.
Materials: warp – jute; weft – wool; pile – wool.
Knots: Sehna, density per sq.cm.: 15—20.
Sizes: length 3.50 m. and smaller rugs 3 × 2 m., 3.50 × 2.40 m. The colour scheme and the patterns resemble the Yomud carpets, often with designs like Bokhara carpets.

Palas. Outstanding work by the Tekke, Turkoman and Yomud tribes.
Material: wool.
Size: 1.90 × 3.00 m.
Colour: predominantly dark chestnut.
Design: woven carpets, patterned on both sides.

Pende (plate 48). Made in the Merv Oasis, near the town of Merv on the Afghan border, by Turkomans, Chiwinzi and Armenians.
Material: wool.
Knots: Sehna, density per sq.cm.: up to 50.
Sizes: 3 × 2 m., 1.00 × 0.80 m., 3.50 × 5.00 m.
Colours: deep red, blue, white and ivory.
Design: the broad borders divided up into narrow stripes are striking; the carpets often have *gul* patterns.

Tekke-Turkoman. Woven in the neighbourhood of Ashkabad and Merv, mainly by women of semi-nomadic tribes, who migrate as far as the northern steppes of Iran. These carpets are widely known in Europe.
Materials: wool; warp – jute.
Knots: Sehna, density per sq.cm.: 30—50.
Sizes: the dimensions are being adapted to European needs, formerly 1.60 × 2.80 m., 0.80 × 1.10 m., now up to 4 × 5 m.
Colours: predominantly red shades ranging from mahogany to the colour of bull's blood.
Design: regularly placed octagons with motifs of tarantulas or conventionalised stars and hooks, and often *gul* designs. The borders included stars, lozenges and geometrical floral designs.

Yomud (plates 42, 43, 46). Made over a vast territory between northern Iran and the Caspian Sea, Uzbekistan and Afghanistan, work of the Yomud nomads.

Materials: wool with animal hair.
Knots: Sehna, density per sq.cm.: 20.
Size: 3 × 2 m.
Colours: predominantly red, ranging from light red to crimson, and white.
Design: chiefly of the *gul* pattern set in horizontal or vertical rows all over the inner field. The border has bird designs, eagles stylised into patterns, foliage, trees, also stylised.

EASTERN TURKESTAN

The work was made predominantly by Chinese weavers, and also by Tartars and Manchurians, Kalmyks and the Kirghiz. Although there is a long tradition of carpet-making in this area, it has not been studied in detail and so the different types of carpet are difficult to classify.

Proofs of the very early existence of woven carpets were collected by the Turfan expedition of the Berlin Museum and by the explorer Sir Aurel Stein. Around the year 1900 these carpets began to find their way in larger numbers via Istanbul into international trade. On the market they were known as Samarkand or Margelan carpets, and not named after the places where they were actually produced. All carpets from the area show Turkoman influences, particularly in their simple, geometrical designs. They are made of fine, glossy wool, often with silk, or gold and silver threads.

Kashgar. Production in the town of Kashgar, the most western town of China. The carpets are technically identical to those made at Yarkand, with Chinese elements noticeable in the design.

Khotan. The town lies on an important caravan route from India to Kashgar.
Materials: mainly silk; warp – cotton; weft and pile – wool.
Knots: Ghiordes and Sehna, density per sq.cm.: 3—5.
Sizes: 0.90—1.10 × 1.50—2.50 m., 1.30—2.00 × 2.50—4.50 m.
Colours: strikingly deep shades, with pink and brick red, dark blue, white and golden yellow as the main colours.
Design: shows Chinese motifs, stems covered in blossom, flower vases, meanders, naturalistically depicted animals (bats, butterflies), the tree of life and whole landscapes. The carpets often have a central medallion formed by the circle of happiness set against a plain ground with swastikas. Meanders and large rosettes frequently appear on the borders.

Samarkand. The town was a collecting centre for carpets made in a large area from Khotan to Kashgar.
Materials: warp – wool or cotton; weft and pile – wool.
Knots: Sehna, density per sq.cm.: 6—8.
Size: runners or carpets up to a length of 4 m.
Colours: all the conceivable shades of yellow, also blue, pink, crimson.
Design: the field has three medallions or is completely covered in regularly placed patterns. The border usually has the meander design.

Yarkand. Produced in the town of Yarkand, on the road from India to Kashgar, and an important centre of trade.
Materials: wool, occasionally silk.
Knots: Sehna.
Size: 2 × 4 m.
Colours: limited to dark blue or medium dark mahogany red, with white to grey or yellow ground.

AFGHANISTAN (plate 50)

The carpets made in this part were the work of the Turkoman nomads who migrated as far as the northern borders of Afghanistan. The great interest shown in such carpets in Europe and the large size, up to 4 × 5 m., caused a decline of quality which is observable after about 1900. The older carpets are made of silk, the more recent ones of wool and goat hair. There is a great difference in the quality between washed and unwashed carpets, so that most of them reached Europe after cleaning.

Old Afghan. Produced in the vicinity of the towns of Kabul and Herat, where they were collected.
Material: wool with animal hair.
Knots: Sehna, density per sq.cm.: 10—15.
Size: runners and large carpets up to 5.50 m. long.
Colours: predominantly warm red, with blue, light red and white in the pattern.
Design: restful, geometrical, using the *gul* motif set in a regular design. The broad border has up to six stripes, barber's poles, and zig-zag patterns, hour-glass motifs.

Modern Afghan. Technically identical with the Old Afghan carpets, although the quality of work differs greatly. The pattern with its regular rows has white octagons both in the main field and the border.

Ennessi (*kachli, kach* = cross [Armenian]). These carpets with the cross patterns (see p. 16) were made by Christian weavers, otherwise they do not differ from other Afghan carpets. They are used as door hangings.

Kabul. The carpets made in the town of Kabul came on to the world market between 1890 and 1900, and then disappeared completely. Being soft, they were used mainly as hangings.
Materials: wool, often combined with silk (used to weave the *gul* pattern).
Knots: Sehna.
Size: 1.40 × 2.90 m.
Colours: copper red, dark blue, patterns in brown, green, orange-yelllow. The borders are cream-coloured or white.
Design: the *gul* motif appears frequently, rows of octagons, and an elephant's foot pattern. The carpets which were to be sent to markets in Italy and England have a golden sheen achieved by chemicals.

BELUCHISTAN (plates 47, 49)

The area of this name lies to the east of Iran and south of Afghanistan and today forms part of western Pakistan; the town of Meshed in north-western Iran was the collecting centre. The carpets were made by ten nomad tribes, especially those in the Khorasan area; each uses slightly different patterns, but the colours of all of them are mainly brown and white. There are great differences in quality between the carpets of the nomads and those of settled inhabitants. For a long time these carpets remained unknown in Europe.

Beluch. The carpet-makers were Beluch nomads who migrated with their flocks from the region of Meshed to the Persian Gulf.
Materials: warp – wool and animal hair, sometimes jute; weft – goat hair or wool; pile – wool.
Knots: Sehna, density per sq.cm.: 10—15.

Sizes: 0.80 × 1.20 m., 1.20 × 2.10 m., 1.50 × 2.00 m.

Colours: predominantly dark red and brown, sometimes blue and white, hardly ever yellow.

Design: geometrical patterns of highly stylised flowers, which fill the central field in diagonal stripes. The term Meshed-Beluch was given to all small carpets of the area distributed through the town of Meshed.

Asia Minor, which after 1300 came under Turkish domination, had a flourishing tradition of carpet-making dating far back to antiquity. Greek historians speak of weavers of carpets and dyers of wool. The oldest surviving carpets date from the period of 1200 to 1300 A.D., and, though only a small number exist now, they provide proof of wide-scale production. Their ornamentation is strictly geometrical; Byzantine-Sassanian influences are apparent in the motifs: circular patterns, shields, with animals, Kufic script along the border. In 1283, when it was under the rule of the Seljuks, Marco Polo reported that the most beautiful carpets in the world were made in Konya.

It is very difficult to determine the provenance of these old carpets; most of them were made in the provinces of Ankara and Konya, under both Persian and Caucasian influences. During the thirteenth and fourteenth centuries trade between Turkey and Venice, Genoa and Florence flourished and many paintings of this period show carpets from Asia Minor which are very similar to the surviving fragments. Examples can be seen in pictures by Giotto: The *Stephaneschi Polyptych* (the Vatican Gallery, Rome); Fra Angelico: *The Madonna with SS Cosmos and Damian* (the Accademia, Florence); Lippo Memmi: *Madonna* (Berlin Gallery). They reveal not only Sassanian and Byzantine influence, but also traces of Moorish-Spanish designs, which must have been copied directly. They formed a predecessor to the so-called Armenian animal carpets, which reached a culminating point at the time of the Safavids.

After about 1500 the weavers of Asia Minor began to adopt Persian patterns and during the seventeenth century, once Persian designs had stopped developing and had become static, they spread throughout the Middle East.

Old Luxury Carpets. Made in workshops near the towns of Bursa and Istanbul under Persian influence, and, as in Persia, they were made for the court and the nobility. The very few which have survived are made of wool and silk. They are softer than the Persian carpets and were used frequently as hangings, covers, etc.

Syrian Carpets. The name does not mark the provenance and they have nothing in common with Syrian art. These large carpets must have been made in some Turkish court factory near Istanbul or Bursa.

Materials: woven of silk or angora wool.

Colours: nearly always include cherry red and shades of brown; the rest of the pattern is in blue, green, red, black and white.

Design: Persian ornaments are used, but with more medallions, and with rosettes and tendrils, covered with narcissus blossom, hyacinths and tulips. The overpowering effect of the ornaments point to a time when the classical form had been abandoned.

Damascus. The carpets that bear this name were not necessarily made in Damascus; they may well have been produced in Morocco or Spain, or in some court factory in Istanbul. But it is possible that Damascus was the centre of the trade. Carpets of this kind, known as *tapeti damaschini*, are often shown in sixteenth-century Venetian paintings.

Materials: angora wool and silk.

Colours: bright and multi-coloured against a cherry red ground, with light green and blue in the design.
Design: some carpets have geometrical patterns set out like a kaleidoscope, with a central motif of a multi-pointed star. Others have naturalistic ornaments, with rich motifs, which resemble the designs on Damascus and Rhodes faience of the sixteenth and seventeenth centuries.

Chintamani. A group of carpets woven of rather rough wool which repeat *chintamani* motifs in regular patterns (see *Glossary of Ornaments*, p. 16). Their frequent appearance in Asia Minor is explained by the fact that Timur, who bore this design on his coat of arms, conquered the Turks.

Ushak (plate 60). These luxury old carpets influenced by Persia were probably made between 1500 and 1750 at Smyrna and in the surrounding area. Carpets of this design can be found in pictures of all those countries to which Oriental carpets were exported, in works by, for instance Velasquez, Vermeer, Bordone, etc. The oldest record is a picture ordered by Queen Elizabeth of England in 1570, which shows the family of Henry VII.
Colours: the background is a predominantly warm dark blue shade, the border brick red. The motifs are made in light yellow, various shades of green, light blue, red and white.
Design: the composition consists of an oval medallion in the centre with stylised Persian flower tendrils and cloud-bands. More recent carpets have simpler designs. The borders have three stripes, with flowers along the central one, and geometrical motifs along the edge.

'Holbein' carpets. Although named after the painters Holbein, the earliest representation of these carpets can be found on a work of 1520 by Lorenzo Lotto. Other examples can be found in paintings by Longhi, Bronzino, Brueghel, Francken, Terborch, Carpaccio, Ghirlandaio and painters from all the countries to which Oriental carpets were exported. By the end of the seventeenth century their depiction ceased altogether.
Colours: varied, highly expressive schemes with dark red grounds and blue borders.
Design: angular forms of tendrils, arabesques, Kufic script, later floral designs, lattice-work and cloud-bands. During the seventeenth century the ornamentation of the inner field became sparser. These carpets are often found in the form of prayer rugs.

Transylvanian carpets. When a large number of these carpets were found in the churches at Kronstadt in Transylvania, the name became attached to all carpets of the kind. They are also often found in churches in Hungary, Poland, Italy and Germany.
Size: 1.20 × 2.00 m.
Colours: strikingly pure, with brick red as ground, and yellow, dark blue and green patterns, occasionally dark red and ivory colour.
Design: resembles that of the Ushak carpets, with a vase, flowers and leaves in the centre and arabesques at the corners. Later examples (1520—1700) were copies of old Persian carpets.

Semi-Antique and Modern Carpets from Asia Minor

Anatolian Prayer Rugs. Between 1880 and 1890 many carpets, probably made in various regions such as Angora and Konya, came to Europe under this name.
Materials: wool and goat hair; rather loose weave.

Knots: Ghiordes.
Size: 0.80 × 1.30 m.

Anatolian Runners. This name is attached to high quality carpets from Asia Minor where the precise place of origin is not known.
Materials: wool and goat hair.
Knots: Ghiordes.
Colours: frequently red, blue, green, cream.
Design: often have designs of towers both in the central field and the border, also minarets and palms.

Bandirma (plate 56). Produced in northern Turkey, in the town of that name situated on the shores of the Sea of Marmara. Made in large quantities, these carpets are not of outstanding quality, and used as hangings rather than floor coverings.
Materials: warp – cotton; weft – cotton; pile – wool, cotton, sometimes a mixture of cotton and silk.
Knots: Density per sq.cm.: 15—25.
Sizes: 2.50 × 3.50 m., or smaller.
Colours: blue, red, ivory, with up to twelve colours in the pattern.
Design: features from all other types of prayer rugs, mainly Kula or Persian in origin.

Bergama (plate 54). The town is situated to the north of Smyrna. The carpets were made by nomads in western and southern Anatolia.
Materials: warp and weft – wool, sometimes with goat hair; pile – soft wool.
Knots: Ghiordes, density per sq.cm.: 8—12.
Sizes: nearly all the carpets are almost square: 0.80 × 1.10 m., 2 × 3 m.
Colours: the ground is mainly blue and cherry red, sometimes light green, the pattern shows yellow, orange and often ivory tones.
Design: resemble Turkoman carpets with geometrical designs of squares, stars, diamonds. Mainly used as prayer rugs.

Bursa. Produced in northern Turkey, mainly as prayer rugs. Bursa is situated 30 km. from the Sea of Marmara. These are poor quality, short pile carpets, except for a short period after the First World War, and they lose their gloss very rapidly.
Materials: warp and weft – cotton; pile – silk mixed with cotton.
Knots: Ghiordes, density per sq.cm.: 18—25.
Sizes: small dimensions.
Colours: blue, red and ivory form the basic colours.
Design: the borders often have Herati patterns of floral motifs, usually in three stripes.

Ghiordes (plate 53, 57, 61). The older of these carpets are among the highest quality to have been made in Turkey, the more recent ones are less good. These densely woven, short pile carpets are produced in northern Turkey, in the town of Ghiordes, north-east of Smyrna.
Materials: warp – cotton or wool; weft – wool; pile – wool.
Knots: Ghiordes, density per sq.cm.: 30—50.
Sizes: 1.30 × 2.20 m., 1.10 × 1.60 m.
Colours: red, and less frequently blue and green.
Design: mainly prayer rugs with two columns, a lamp hanging from the mihrab (the pointed design at one end of a prayer rug), and flowers or vases with flowers. The border is divided into three stripes with the Herati pattern in the central one, and flowers along the edges.

Hereke. Before the First World War the town of Hereke in north-western Turkey had a large factory producing high quality carpets with a Frenchman in charge of the designs.
Materials: silk and wool.
Knots: Ghiordes, density per sq.cm.: 20—40.
Sizes: 2 × 3 m., up to 5 × 8 m.
Colours: the ground is mainly white or beige.
Design: this ranges from copies of luxury Persian carpets and prayer rugs, often with medallions, landscapes and animals and people, to relief carpets with short pile in the style of Louis XV and XVI. In about 1900 Art Nouveau patterns were used; Sultan Abdul Hamid had Art Nouveau carpets made to decorate certain of the rooms of his palace at Istanbul.

Kis-Ghiordes. Made in the town which lies to the north-east of Smyrna. Small, almost square carpets of the Bergama type, using medallions in the pattern with step-like frames on a blue ground. Used as gifts to bridegrooms.

Konya (plate 51). Production, which has now ceased, of central Turkey.
Materials: warp – cotton; weft – wool or goat hair; pile – wool.
Knots: Ghiordes, density per sq.cm.: 10—14.
Sizes: rugs and small carpets at most 3 m. long, 1.15 × 1.80 m.
Colours: white, beige, red and blue.
Design: geometrical, with two or three medallions in the shape of a hectagon or lozenge with a narrow border, naturalistic flowers, Rhodes lilies.

Kula (plates 52, 57, 59). A small town in central Turkey south-east of Ghiordes. Most of the carpets are prayer rugs, the older of them made of very good quality wool, but are relatively soft.
Materials: warp – wool or cotton; weft – wool or goat hair; pile – wool.
Knots: Ghiordes, density per sq.cm.: 8—15.
Size: 1.15 × 1.80 m.
Colours: red, blue, less frequently beige, with a brightly-coloured pattern.
Design: the centres of the carpets are formed by lozenge-shaped medallions framed in step-like borders. The borders often have alligator patterns or large stylised flowers. The 'cemetery Kula' is a carpet with a pattern of stylised cypress trees.

Ladik (plate 55). Today an insignificant town in central Turkey, formerly famous for its production of prayer rugs. The older carpets are of high quality, but more recent ones are only average.
Materials: warp – wool or cotton; weft and pile – wool.
Knots: Ghiordes, density per sq.cm.: 10—20.
Sizes: 1 × 1.80 m., 1.40 × 2 m.
Basic colours: red or blue, yellow, cream, green.
Design: the central field is usually set with a tulip design, the border has one broad and several narrower stripes. Pomegranates and stylised trees are frequently used as motifs.

Makri. The town of Makri (Megris) served as collecting centre for carpets, most of which were produced on the island of Rhodes as prayer rugs. They came on to the European market mainly between 1890 and 1900.
Material: wool, long shiny pile, densely woven.
Knots: Ghiordes, density per sq.cm.: 7—10.
Size: 1 × 1.70 m.
Basic colours: red, blue, yellow, green.

Design: resembles a church window divided into three panels pointed at the top, and sometimes also at the bottom.

Melas. The town of Melas, lying to the south of Smyrna, not far from the Mediterranean coast, is a collecting centre for carpets from western Turkey. The oldest carpets date back to between 1750 and 1800.
Materials: warp – wool, cotton or goat hair; weft and pile – wool.
Knots: Ghiordes, density per sq.cm.: 6—10.
Size: 0.90 × 1.40 m.
Basic colours: include copper, light red, blue or green. The borders are bright golden-yellow, dark blue, yellow, brown, less frequently green.
Design: the patterns resemble Caucasian designs, with stripes and zig-zags, often with a large medallion in the central field. The border has three stripes, with flowers in the central one. The prayer rugs have a patternless mihrab.

Mohair. Derived its name from mohair wool, which from 1895 onwards was made in the province of Aidin. The goats which provided wool were kept mainly in the provinces of Angora and Konya.
Material: goat wool.
Knots: Ghiordes.
Sizes: 2.50 × 3.50 m., 3 × 4 m.
Colours: bright, chiefly pink, light blue, dark red and dark blue shades.
Design: no typical designs – some features of all other carpets from Asia Minor.

Mujur. Production of prayer rugs in the town of Mujur on the Kizil Irmak river in central Turkey; carpets were known as *Namyslyk* carpets, the Turkish name for 'prayer rugs'.
Materials: wool, cotton, goat hair. Short glossy wool.
Knots: Ghiordes, density per sq.cm.: 7—10.
Sizes: 1 × 1.60 m., 1.25 × 1.90 m.
Basic colours: red, less often blue or cream, green, with yellow in the border.
Design: resembles Ghiordes carpets, with a stylised tree of life, and columns in the inner field, one main and several minor stripes in the border.

Silk Saph. This name was given to family prayer rugs originally made at Ushak, later in Chinese Turkestan, and then for export purposes in Turkey.
Materials: wool, cotton or silk.
Knots: density per sq.cm.: wool: 12—20; mixed materials: 20—30; silk carpets: 30—50.
Size: 0.90—1 m. × 3.50 m.
Colours: the five to twelve fields are ivory, gold, blue, red, green.

Smyrna. Carpets were probably never actually produced in the town itself, which however was always an important trade centre; wool was traded and spun here, and carpets were collected from the entire province of Aidin for sale to Europe and America. Orders were received for carpets to be made for European taste. They were highly popular from the middle to the end of the nineteenth century. All the carpets were produced in factories; they are rather loosely woven and have a pile of 1—2 cm.
Materials: warp – cotton; weft and pile – wool.
Knots: Ghiordes and Sehna, density per sq.cm.: 2—5.
Sizes: 2—6 m. in width, 2—12 m. in length.
Design: Persian type with a great variety of colours and patterns made to order. Medallions, large flowers, red, green, blue.

Smyrna-Lavé. From the province of Aidin made as new luxury carpets of fine wool, very densely and finely woven with Sehna knots. They are copies of Persian carpets, mostly Tabriz designs, and, in more recent times, also of Chinese carpets.

Sparta. These poor quality carpets were made along the Turkish coast of the Mediterranean; they are loosely woven with a high pile.
Materials: warp – cotton; weft and pile – wool.
Knots: Ghiordes, density per sq.cm.: 6—10.
They exist in various sizes, mainly in pastel shades without a characteristic pattern. Although not particularly attractive, they were popular in Europe from the middle of the nineteenth until the early twentieth centuries.

Sultan. Made in eastern Turkey in the Ararat region, by nomads and semi-nomadic tribes, today also made in factories.
Materials: warp and weft – wool or goat hair; pile – wool.
Knots: Ghiordes, density per sq.cm.: 6—15.
Sizes: 1 × 1.80 m., 1.40—3 m., mainly runners and small carpets.
Basic colours: include blue, red, mainly bright shades.
Design: resembles the Caucasian patterns, with geometrical shapes and step-like edges.

Ushak (plate 60). Made in the town of Ushak in western Turkey.
Materials: warp – cotton; weft – wool or goat hair; pile – wool.
Knots: Ghiordes, density per sq.cm.: 4—10.
Sizes: 0.90 × 1.30 m., 4 × 5 m.
Colours: the older carpets have only three colours – dark green, dark blue and dark red, but after 1750 more colours were used.
Design: the modern carpets adapt ancient Ushak patterns.

CAUCASUS

The relatively small region in which Caucasian carpets were made is bordered by the Black and Caspian Seas and inhabited by people of various nationalities. The colourful history of the area, where the rule passed from dynasty to dynasty, began with the Old Testament story of the cradle of mankind on Mount Ararat. The nomad tradition of carpet production is long-established and is entirely different in character from that of Persia and Asia Minor. All the tribes – Turkomans, Turks, Persians and Armenians – have been faithful to the conventions of early geometrical designs. The carpets, which to this day accord to the old patterns, are of very good quality material and expertly woven.

Tbilisi (Tiflis) in central Georgia is the centre of contemporary trade, but not of actual production.

Dragon Carpets, fifteenth to seventeenth centuries. These very rare works used to be thought the work of Armenians or Mongols. But in more recent times a direct connection with the local Scythian culture has been shown. This theory is further supported by discoveries of old carpets in the Altai region.

The designs show typical heraldic patterns with double animal bodies, mainly dragons, particularly combats between dragons and phoenixes, which in all Asiatic art had a mythical, symbolic meaning. Typical features include a narrow border with wavy tendril motifs and stylised lilies, pointed leaves or rosettes. In the course of the sixteenth century, under the influence of the advance of Islam, the animal motifs gradually gave way to floral designs.

The average density of knots is 30 to 1 sq.cm. The carpets are strikingly coloured, using up to ten shades on a ground of red, dark blue or dark brown.

Baku. Produced on the shores of the Caspian Sea near the town of Baku (called Shemakha until 1859) in the village of Amer-Adshan.

44

Materials: wool, camel hair, cotton.
Knots: Ghiordes, density per sq.cm.: 25.
Sizes: 1.50 × 1.80 m., 2 × 4 m.
Colours: dull broken tones as if faded in the sun, light green, a wide range of shades of blue, light yellow, with dark blue or black ground.
Design: the centre of the pattern is formed by a large star-shaped medallion with four corner sectors. The borders with three stripes and geometrical motifs include conventionalised human and animal figures.

Chichi (Tzitzi). Made by the Chichi tribes of the north-western borders of Daghestan, in parts of the Terek region.
Materials: soft wool with a short pile.
Knots: Ghiordes, density per sq.cm.: 14.
Size: 1.00 × 1.40 m.
Colours: ivory, red, brown, orange and a dark blue ground.
Design: the inner field is divided into a mosaic by small geometrical patterns, sometimes spiral or floral motifs set in rows. The border has three or six stripes with rosettes.

Daghestan. Made on the western shores of the Caspian Sea in the northern Caucasus. Some experts sometimes call these carpets Lesghistan after the Lesghi tribe which lived in the region to the north of Kuba in the Daghestan district.
Materials: warp – cotton; weft – wool or cotton; pile – wool.
Knots: Ghiordes, density per sq.cm.: 8—20.
Sizes: 0.80 × 1.40 m., 1 × 1.70 m., 1.15 × 2.80 m., the largest are up to 3.50 m. long.
Colours: the undyed wool, frequently used, is white or brown; sometimes it is blue or red.
Design: the central field and the border show small square-shaped patterns sited in length or crosswise stripes. The border often has trefoil, wine glass, barbers' pole, conventionalised flower or arrow motifs. Sometimes a stylised eagle's head or geometrical designs with step-like edges are used.

Derbend (plate 64). The town of Derbend served as trade centre for carpets made in the surrounding mountains on the western shores of the Caspian Sea.
Materials: warp – cotton, weft – wool, cotton or sometimes undyed goat hair; pile – wool.
Knots: Ghiordes, density per sq.cm.: 8—12.
Sizes: 1.40 × 2.50 m., 1.70 × 3.50 m.
Colours: dark blue, less often red was used as ground colour, with motifs in yellow, green, white, and a white background in the border.
Design: the central field has one to three medallions, the main part of the border is decorated with stars, squares, arrow points and triangles.

Gendje. Today called Kirovabad, the collecting centre for carpets from the Armenian Caucasus.
Materials: warp – wool or goat hair, sometimes cotton; weft – wool or goat hair; pile – wool.
Knots: Ghiordes, density per sq.cm.: 8—12.
Sizes: 0.80 × 1.60 m., 1.20 × 4.00 m.
Colours: include beige, red or blue, otherwise the colour scheme is bright. Poor quality dyes were used.
Design: resembles that of Kazak and has small motifs of stars, squares, etc., often set in rows.

Karabagh. Carpets from the southern Caucasus or the northern borders of the Kurdish steppes.

Materials: warp – cotton; weft and pile – wool. Rough wool with a short pile.
Knots: Ghiordes, density per sq.cm.: 8—15.
Sizes: 0.70×0.90 m., 1.10×1.40 m.
Colours: typical colours included cochineal red, or occasionally blue.
Design: the gently rounded geometrical patterns are strongly influenced by Persia. The central field has two or three medallions with stylised flowers and animals. Sometimes these carpets were confused with those of Kazak.

Karaje or **Karadagh.** Carpets of glossy wool of good and lasting quality from the southern Caucasus and the area stretching to the northern borders of the Kurdish steppe.
Materials: warp – cotton; weft – wool or goat hair; pile – wool.
Knots: Ghiordes, density per sq.cm.: 15—19.
Sizes: small runners or carpets up to 3 m. long.
Basic colours: red or blue.
Design: includes both Caucasian motifs, large stars, squares with step-shaped edges, but also eastern Asian and Persian elements: flowers, the Herati design.

Kazak. The producers of these carpets were mostly nomad Kazaks, Cherkess, Armenians and Kurds of the central Caucasus.
Materials: warp – wool or cotton; weft and pile – wool. Sometimes goat hair was used in the warp and camel hair in the pile.
Knots: Ghiordes, density per sq.cm.: 13—20, 8—18.
Sizes: 0.90×1.30 m., 1.60×2.20 m., 0.70×1.00 m., the biggest up to 3.50 m. in length.
Basic colours: mainly red and blue, less often ivory, with green, yellow, sometimes pink and brown in the pattern. The border is ivory or cream coloured.
Design: follows strict geometrical shapes, with an octagonal, star-shaped or cross medallion in the central field, inset with conventionalised floral or animal designs, camels or birds, for instance. The border is composed of five stripes with motifs of wine glasses, crabs, barbers' poles, zig-zags, S-shapes, stars. Sometimes there is a pattern similar to a cloud-band.

Kuba (plate 63). Most of the population of Kuba, which lies on the shores of the Caspian Sea between Derbend and Baku, is engaged in carpet production and the town is an important trade centre for the area. The carpets are among the highest quality to come from the Caucasus.
Materials: warp – cotton or wool; weft and pile – wool.
Knots: Ghiordes, density per sq.cm.: 10—15.
Size: small runners or carpets up to 3 m. in length.
Colours: the ground is dark red or dark blue, sometimes beige.
Designs: geometrical and two to three stripes with S-shapes along the border.

Lesghistan. Carpets from the western Caucasus, the eastern shores of the Black Sea.
Materials: warp – cotton or wool; weft and pile – wool.
Knots: Ghiordes, density per sq.cm.: 10—15.
Sizes: 1.00×1.40 m., 1.40×3.50 m.
Colours: light brilliant blue, red, beige as basic colours.
Design: shows influence of Oriental patterns, most often in the star motifs, rosettes, and squares with step-shaped edges and hooks.

Moghan. Carpets similar to those from Shirvan from the Moghan steppe near Talish.

Materials: warp – cotton or wool; weft and pile – wool.
Knots: Ghiordes, density per sq.cm.: 8—20.
Size: 1.20×1.80 m.
Colours: include cochineal red ranging to purple.
Design: small medallions surrounded by flowers in the central field.

Old Shirvan (plates 65, 66). The Shirvan district had a large-scale production of carpets in the old tradition.
Materials: warp – cotton, wool; weft and pile – wool.
Knots: Ghiordes, density per sq.cm.: 8—20.
Sizes: 0.80×1.25 m., 1.20×1.80 m.
Colours: very harmonious, with blue, ivory or red as basic colours, and yellow, pink, light blue in the pattern. Ivory colour along the border.
Design: geometrical with lozenges, octagons, S-motifs; the border, composed of three to five stripes, has wineglasses, scorpions, stars and sometimes a ram's horn pattern.

Modern Shirvan. Carpets are now made in state enterprises where they lack any features of individual production.
Materials: rough wool.
Knots: Ghiordes, density per sq.cm.: 9—20.
Sizes: 0.70×0.90 m., 1.10×1.70 m., the largest up to 3.50 m. long.
Colours: the overall scheme is not harmonious, the tones are brownish, purple to cherry, bluish, yellow and dirty white.
Design: the field is frequently divided into three squares radiating from a point with small geometrical designs. The border is broad, often with wineglass motifs.

Seichur. Carpets from the south-western Caucasus, from the remote and inaccessible mountain areas north of Tbilisi.
Materials: warp – cotton or wool; weft and pile – wool.
Knots: Ghiordes, density per sq.cm.: 10—18.
Sizes: runners or carpets up to 3 m. in length, or 0.90×1.60 m., 1.20×3.50 m.
Colours: bright, mainly blue, red, brown and ivory.
Design: the border tends to be broader than the inner field with lozenge design. The field is divided into two lengthwise stripes with geometrical patterns.

Soumak (Shemakha). The producers of these carpets were nomads in the Shirvan region of the Derbend province.
Materials: wool, woven without pile (the only woven carpets from the Caucasus).
Sizes: 1.80×2.70 m., 0.80×1.30 m., 2×3 m., 2.50×3.50 m.
Colours: the older carpets are a shining brick red, with yellow and blue in the drawing. The contours are bottle green, and in more recent products brown-red with dark blue, sharp green or bright yellow motifs.
Design: large motifs often conventionalised knots of fate, with the border divided into three or five stripes, often with the running-dog motif.

Talish. Made in the region of Baku on the Caspian Sea.
Materials: wool, cotton, goat hair.
Knots: Ghiordes, density per sq.cm.: 8—15.
Sizes: 1.20×2.50 m., 1.30×3 m.
Colours: blue ground, sometimes yellow, the white ground in the border covered with a bright pattern.
Design: the central field is either of a single colour or has a row of stars or

lozenges. The borders have designs of crabs, arrows, running-dogs, zig-zags, often reminiscent of Kazak patterns.

ARMENIA

ARMENIA AND KURDISTAN

The prehistory of what is now Armenia is known to us from the stories of the Old Testament. This was an area where numerous battles were fought, where Persian, Roman, and Byzantine armies marched. It became a great empire where art and architecture flourished and where weaving was known as early as in 700 A. D.

Governed by Persia after 1472, the country was brought into contact with the highly developed Persian civilisation; Shah Abbas summoned Armenians to the Persian weavers' shops in 1603 and Shah Nadir employed them on building sites. When Persian domination gave way to the rule of the Turks, and when, after the beginning of the First World War, Armenia was divided between Russia, Persia and Turkey, carpet production came under these different influences also.

Modern Armenian Carpets. One type is characterised by highly primitive, stylised, symmetrical pairs of animals. By the side of these a second group of carpets exists which shows the strong influence of Persian designs, with fewer stylised elements and very fine treatment. The endeavour to achieve technical finesse is reminiscent of the attempts of Baroque Gobelin tapestries to give the effect of a painting. Contact with almost all the well-known cultures of eastern Asia explains the use of the east Asian motifs of legendary animals, Mongolian escutcheon creatures, the symbols of the Ming dynasty and floral designs.

Sivas. The town in Turkish Asia was, until the First World War, a collecting centre for a highly developed factory and cottage carpet industry. The producers were Armenians, nomads, semi-nomads, and the carpets are sold as from Asia Minor or Anatolia. Production declined after 1900.
Material: wool.
Knots: Ghiordes, density per sq.cm.: 8—12.
Sizes: 2×3 m., 2.50×3.50 m., 3×4 m., less often 3.50×4.50 m. and larger.
Colour: similar to Persian luxury carpets but brighter and fresher.
Design: High quality carpets imitated the patterns on the luxury Persian carpets, particularly Tabriz.

Urfa. Carpets from the ancient town of Edessa in southern Mesopotamia, east of the central Euphrates. The producers were chiefly German factory owners who settled in the town of Urfa between 1900 and 1910. The designs imitate old Oriental patterns.

KURDISTAN (plates 67—74)

Most of Kurdistan, the region between Persia and Asia Minor, was dominated by the Persian Empire, although small areas were under Turkey. The area has a long tradition of carpet-making, which flourished particularly between 1890 and 1900 when large numbers of carpets reached Europe under the name of Yuruk. Today few such carpets reach the trade.

Yuruk. The producers are Kurdish tribes, of partly Iranian, partly Caucasian origin.
Materials: wool, often dark goat hair, so that the fringes are black.
Knots: Ghiordes, density per sq.cm.: 6—14.
Sizes: 1×2 m., 1.15×2.60 m., 1.30×3 m.

Colours: copper-red, grass-green, dark blue, bright yellow, pure white.
Design: rather primitive motifs, geometrical designs often subdivide the central field into crosswise stripes, with star or cross-shaped patterns in the centre. The borders tend to be narrow. These carpets closely resemble Caucasian carpets; they can sometimes be distinguished only by their softer and glossier wool.

CHINA

Europe, which has long been accustomed to Chinese objects, knew practically nothing of **Chinese** carpets until 1900. After the Boxer Rebellion, they began to be imported and after 1920 came to Europe and America in large numbers.

Carpet-making dates back to the period of the Sung dynasty in China (960 to 1279) when luxury carpets were made in northern China. They adopted the patterns already in use in silk materials, ceramics, lacquer work and other forms of craftsmanship. A symbolical meaning, frequently based on Confucian, Taoist or Buddhist precepts, was attached to most of the motifs employed.

In 1275 Marco Polo recorded the existence of factories in Cambulac. The oldest carpets that have survived date back to the Ming dynasty (1368—1644). They are often made of silk, sometimes combined with threads of precious metal, and the pile is clipped or bevelled around the pattern to increase its prominence.

During K'ang Hsi's reign (1662—1722) certain naturalistic features were introduced: floral motifs, and entire landscapes with birds; Imperial gold, a golden-yellow, is the predominant colour.

During Yung Cheng's reign (1723—1735) the decoration became richer and the predominant yellow changed to a lemon yellow shade.

During Ch'ien Lung's reign (1736—1796) the scope of decorative features became even greater to include symbols of science, music and ethics, scrolls, lyres, symbols of power, vases, fans, etc., while the influence of Persian and Indian art introduced a series of naturalistic flowers. Blue and red patterns or dark terracotta with yellow appear generally on a white background.

The dimensions of the carpets are further aids to dating: the oldest carpets are small, even 2×3 m. is exceptionally large. Most of the carpets were either square or oval, or they served as chair covers, etc. The newer carpets are of the following dimensions: 0.80×1.30 m., 2×3 m., 2.50×3.50 m., 3×4 m., and even larger.

The basic scheme of composition of **Chinese** carpets is almost always one-coloured in the central field with a medallion and corner motifs, derived in shape from the central medallion. The border often has the T-motif and meanders. Those made after 1910 were adapted to European and American taste and their dimensions to European needs; they continued to be of very high quality and were mainly made of wool with a high pile cut in plastic shapes.

PAKISTAN

In western Pakistan bordering on Iran and Afghanistan to the west, Kashmir to the north, India to the east and the Arabian Sea to the south, the inhabitants are predominantly Muslim. Production increased substantially after the Second World War when Muslim weavers moved from India to western Pakistan.

The type of carpets known as **Numdah** were woven and knotted, sometimes even embroidered on a felt base. The basic colours are cream or black, with flower and animal designs.

Bokhara carpets were produced in the areas of the carpet industry at Karachi, Lahore and Hyderabad, where they also copied Turkoman, Persian and Caucasian designs. All the carpets are made of wool and cotton, knotted in Sehna knots set very densely.

INDIA   The oldest carpets made in India are thought to have been made under the Mongol Emperor Akbar (1556—1605) and Shah Janangir (1605—1627). At that time Persian craftsmen were summoned to the court at Lahore and Persian decoration, especially of the Kerman and Herati type, had such a strong influence that these carpets are often labelled as Indo-Persian. But it is far easier to distinguish the origin of these carpets than that of many others. Indian decoration is always more naturalistic than Persian: the branches of trees on Persian carpets, although covered with foliage and blossom, always stick straight up while on Indian carpets they bend down. Persian vegetation is always shown in spring time, while Indian shows the trees in summer or autumn. In contrast with Persian carpets, Indian carpets are less densely covered with pattern and the single-coloured background is allowed to show more.

The material used for the carpets is the best Kashmir wool, and occasionally silk in the warp.

After 1850 the export of Indian carpets to Europe expanded. The great demand made it possible for carpets to be made to order according to selected patterns, so that any specific features of Indian production vanished. Some luxury Indian carpets were designed by French or Venetian artists.

Modern production is, on the whole, insignificant. The carpets are made of poor quality materials, are loosely woven and mass production has brought a drop in prices.

JAPAN   Carpets, which were made in Japan from the seventeenth century, were intended for the rich and not for export, although between 1895 and 1910 a few carpets appeared in the trade. Made of hemp, cotton, jute, and occasionally of wool, they were loosely woven, of low quality, and imitated European and Chinese patterns.

SPAIN   For some time Spanish carpets were closely related to Oriental carpets. At the time of the Arab domination of Spain during the twelfth century, cheap Caucasian carpets were imported and served as patterns for subsequent work. Later, in the fifteenth century, carpets brought from Asia Minor were also copied and certain of their motifs were replaced by figurative designs and Kufic script. After 1500 Oriental ornaments gave way to those of the European Renaissance.

The main centre of production was Murcia where carpets with the coats of arms of the Spanish nobility were produced.

In the eighteenth century factories were established on the pattern of the Savonnerie in France.

AFRICA   African carpets which are made both by the Arab and the Berber populations are fairly easily distinguished. Arab work shows the strong influence of Persia; the use of simple ornaments such as volutes, meanders, spirals, stylised tendrils, always tends to be curved or gently rounded. Berber work, on the other hand, with its typical motifs of diamonds and triangles, and step-like toothed edges, uses parallel lines and adheres strictly to rows.

In Africa any work involving wool and weaving was done by women. African wool lacks the finesse and high gloss found in Persia, but it is of good quality. African carpets were never intended for the European market and were exported only on rare occasions.

MOROCCO

Both among the town dwellers and among the Bedouins, carpets formed an essential part of furnishings, providing dignity for important occasions and festivals.

The long, narrow **Atlas** carpets were used for everyday needs, spread on the floor as sleeping mats and as protection from the cold. Very different are **Chleuho** carpets made in the Berber countryside with their geometrical decoration and high pile. The town products, on the other hand, used highly stylised floral motifs.

In 1914 the French attempted to renew the declining carpet industry in Morocco. The main centres of production were Fez, Rabat and Casablanca. The more modern carpets, which closely resemble those from Asia Minor, have sharper colours.

Rabat. The oldest carpets probably date from the eighteenth century.
Material: wool.
Knots: density per sq.cm.: 4.
Colours: very varied, white, red, blue, yellow, green, orange.
Design: highly stylised natural motifs, most of them inspired by carpets from Asia Minor. The central medallion is the shape of a lozenge, outlined by several borders and the entire composition is covered with floral ornaments.

Ait Ighezrane. The work of a Berber tribe, settled about 50 km. from Fez, to the south of the route from Fez to Taza.
Material: wool.
Knots: density per sq.cm.: 4.
Colours: the simple colour scheme is confined to black and white, and a wide range of yellowish and grey tones, and various shades of grey and brown.
Design: the high pile makes the simple geometrical designs of the pattern rather difficult to distinguish.

Ait Seghrushene. The work of a semi-nomad tribe, which migrates in summer to the valleys of Véd Mdez, and in winter to the uplands of Tichoukt.
Material: wool.
Knots: density per sq.cm.: 4.
Colours: black, red and brown.
Design: frequent motifs include a large diamond, made up of two lines of black knots, set into a third outer line of brown knots. Inside this are further diamonds of black and red knots.

Beni Mguild. A large tribe of the Irchlaones (in the region of Azrou and Itzer).
Material: long wool.
Colours: red, chestnut, blue, yellow, orange, green, black, generally with a white ground.
Design: natural motifs in strict stylisation, placed into diamonds of various sizes.

ALGERIA

Djebel-Amour. The producers of these carpets are Arabs at Geriville and Aflou.
Material: long strands of wool.
Colours: dark, mainly indigo tones, sometimes with a little green.
Design: this tends to be very simple, based on geometrical combinations of diamonds.

Guergour. Today factory production, imitating carpets from Asia Minor, mostly with Smyrna patterns.
Material: wool.

Colours: fresh, with a crimson base, and sometimes shades of saffron yellow and golden-green.
Pattern: composed of diamond medallions with tooth edges.

Kalar. Berber work produced at Beni-Rached at Orania.
Material: wool.
Colours: mainly pink shades of henna and green made of oak bark.
Design: strictly geometrical with cross, hook and flower motifs. The pile is cut according to the pattern.

Mzab. Produced at Beni-Isguen and in the Laghouat region.
Material: very fine, densely woven wool.
Colours: mainly red, lichen green and black.
Design: of geometrical lines, lozenges, rectangles, parallel themes set asymmetrically.

TUNISIA

In about 1900 fairly large workshops came into existence in the towns of Kairouan and Gabes and the region between Feriana and Tebessa. The carpets produced there were of good, lasting quality, but were hardly ever sold to Europe.

EGYPT

It is difficult to judge what place carpets took in ancient Egypt, which reached a high standard in all types of textile production. Today, Egypt participates commercially in the production of Oriental carpets: Cairo is a centre from which Persian **Shiraz** carpets are exported, and Suez and Alexandria serve as harbours from which carpets from Persia and Asia Minor are shipped.

Towards the end of the nineteenth century several large exhibitions of Oriental art were held in Europe. In 1873 the World Exhibition in Vienna had a Persian pavilion; in 1891 there was an exhibition of Oriental carpets in Vienna, and in 1910, one of Muslim art in Munich. The interest in Oriental carpets which these engendered was speedily taken up by businessmen who collected carpets first from easily accessible places in the main production and trade centres, and then from more remote regions. Prices were low, because in these poverty stricken areas they had no idea either of the value of the carpets or of money.

Demand increased rapidly, more rapidly than it could be satisfied. Not content with well-preserved carpets, agents acquired damaged and repaired pieces. The fashion for collecting led to mass production, which left its marks both on the quality of the work and the design. Previously many carpets were made and used by the same man, so that they were part of his very existence; now they were made in factories or, if at home, for export.

Today the cost of new carpets is rising with the rising standard of living in the Orient and by virtue of the price ascribed to craftsmanship. Since the end of the Second World War, the main centres of trade in Oriental carpets have been London, Hamburg, Zurich and Stockholm, and Leningrad for Russian and Caucasian carpets.

It must be strongly advised that the most reliable person to buy from is a respectable, perhaps even well-known dealer. Some people prefer the slightly hazardous, but more dramatic business of participating in an auction, but objects should never be purchased from a chance salesman. The carpet must always be examined as a whole, in good light looking along and against the pile, so that its overall condition can be ascertained. There can be great differences, even in two carpets from the same region, in the quality of the material, the weaving and dyes. The density of the work can be discovered by counting the number of knots per square centimetre. The regularity of the knotting can be detected by pushing aside the pile so as to see the ground. Chemically washed carpets are brighter at the knot than in the pile. Discoloured pile is sometimes the result of a burn and in certain places the carpets tend to be thinner. The weft threads show whether the wool has been affected by acid.

A carpet that has had heavy wear often loses its original shape, particularly if it is loosely woven. If there are twists in the warp threads, the carpet will make a sort of cracking sound and has an uneven feeling when stroked lightly with the palm of the hand. In good quality carpets the pile can stand up to the strongest pressure without leaving a noticeable mark. The best test is to put one's full weight on one heel and twist it; the dense, elastic pile of a high quality carpet straightens up immediately, while a clear print is left on a rough Smyrna carpet. The back of the carpet should also be carefully examined, as it points to the quality, density and regularity of the weaving and may reveal additional repairs. A crackling sound when a carpet is rubbed back to back indicates brittle, rotting wool.

Older carpets are obviously more precious than newer ones, even though many of them are damaged, fraying at the edges, and the pile is becoming thin. Such carpets have to be treated with as much care as a fragile painting and should be treated with similar attention and knowledge in the care of a restorer. Damaged parts have to be re-knotted, edges have to be strengthened with supporting strips, and the whole carpet may have to be lined, and new fringes attached. Such a carpet can then no longer be used as a floor covering; it should be hung on a wall attached to a pole spreading its weight evenly.

It is difficult to determine the age of any carpet. The information, which in rare cases is woven into the carpet, is unreliable. Older patterns were copied and often the date plays a purely decorative part. Only old carpets can be correctly dated from contemporary paintings and miniatures and according to the archives and inventories mainly of European churches.

The rate of wear and tear of a carpet is not always a guiding feature in determining age; it is more often the result of the quality of the material and the weaving and the purpose which the carpet served.

The imitation of old patterns of Oriental carpets has been current practice both in the Orient and in Europe over a long period. These carpets were produced without any intention of deceiving the customers; they were simply imitations in usually very good quality material and execution of older, no longer existing, patterns. The possibilities in this were naturally seized upon by speculators who attempted, often with much success, to copy ancient carpets and sell them as originals. Some of the oldest proofs of this practice are the copies of Tabriz carpets which are highly valued in Europe. Often these new carpets were later made to look old, usually without the knowledge of the producers.

After 1900 'antique' carpets known as 'Bandirma' began to appear on the market, and were frequently sold by house-to-house salesmen. The name refers to a town on the southern shores of the Sea of Marmara, from where no historical carpets have survived. They turned out to be good copies of ancient Persian and Asia Minor patterns, carpets made of wool and silk, woven very delicately and with the use of gold and silver threads. The patterns were shaded according to the ancient designs, intentional mistakes were inserted, artificially pierced holes and tears were repaired with the utmost care. Most of them were 1.20 × 2.00 m. in size and in about 1914,1 sq.m. was worth 150 to 300 francs. The carpets were of such high quality that even experienced dealers were deceived and considered them ancient carpets. It was not until a chemical analysis was undertaken that the forgeries came to light. Although the method is not entirely reliable, age of wool can be detected by touch, for the wool of ancient carpets is far more springy and softer and not as dry as the wool of newer carpets.

After weaving, the colours of most Oriental carpets are very bright and have to be subdued if the carpet is to pass as old. This discolouration is carried out in a variety of ways, all of which mean a decline in the quality of the material which is affected by the process. Sometimes the carpet is exposed to the effect of bright sunlight, elsewhere the surface is washed, but mostly chemical means are employed: chloride of lime, acids or lemon juice serve the purpose. After an application of acids the effect has to be neutralized with an alkali substance to prevent the wool from being damaged. An appearance of age is achieved by rubbing in coffee grounds, or by burying the carpet in the ground. Another way used was to spray the surface with alcohol, which is then set alight. In this manner the top of the pile is singed and the carpet receives a softer tone. In some places the entire carpet is seared with a spirit lamp on both sides and the burnt bits brushed off with a hard brush. All these manners of discolouring carpets were first used in Europe and from there found their way to the Orient where they are now common practice.

On the other hand, old carpets are sometimes subject to tricks, too; places that have lost their brilliant colours can be freshened up with water colour paint prior to sale, but it is very simple to discover this.

Where Oriental carpets are in current use in the home, they must be given the normal care and attention devoted to every carpet. They must be placed absolutely flat on the floor and should not be weighed down with heavy pieces of furniture. They should be vacuum-cleaned or lightly brushed at most once a week. Beating may lead to a loosening of the pile and should only be very infrequent. The best method of cleaning is to brush the back of the carpet in dry snow, with light movements, constantly moving to clean patches of snow.

When carpets are not being used for some time, they should be stored, rolled up over a straight pole with the pile inside, wrapped in paper or material and put in a well-aired place. Moth protection should be applied, DDT for example. Spots should be gently rubbed with petrol. For thorough cleaning it is advisable to send the carpet to an expert cleaner where it can be chemically treated, steamed and all the germs destroyed.

LIST OF CARPETS DETERMINED BY SIZES

Charbad	small carpets up to 1.00 by 0.80 m.
Choval	0.80 by 1.60 m. Worked and used in similar manner as Torba carpets.
Dosar	1.30 by 2.10 m.
Kellegi	long, narrow carpet, two or three times as long as wide, example of width 0.70 m.
Keley	1.50—2.00 m. long, and twice as wide.
Kenareh	runner 0.75—1.00 m. wide, 5—6 m. long.
Namaseh	prayer rug 1.00 by 0.80 m.
Poshti	runner 0.60 by 0.90 m.
Quali	1.80 by 2.80 m. and wider.
Sarquart	pieces 1.30 m. long.
Sedshadeh	1.80—2.30 m. by 1.25—1.50 m.
Torba	0.40 by 1.00 m., double, the back is woven, the front knotted. Served as bag for the Nomads.
Yastik	Turkish name for runners 0.25—0.40 by 0.50—0.80 m.
Zarsherek	runner 0.70 by 1.40 m.

1 a, b   Persia, DOSAR. 1.90×1.25 m., 8 knots per sq.cm., first half of the nineteenth century. Private collection, Teheran

2   Persia, HAMADAN. 3.50×0.90 m., 6 knots per sq.cm., camel hair, second half of the nineteenth century. Private collection, Teheran

3 a, b   Persia, TABRIZ. 2.30×1.30 m., 7 knots per sq.cm., beginning of the twentieth century. Private collection, Teheran

4 a, b   Persia, SARUK. 1.90×1.25 m., 8 knots per sq. cm., second half of the nineteenth century. Private collection, Teheran

5   Persia, HAMADAN. 4.00×0.90 m., 6 knots per sq. cm., camel hair, second half of the nineteenth century. Private collection, Teheran

6   Persia, DAULATABAD. Prayer carpet, 1.60×1.85 m. Private collection, Kabul

7 a, b   Persia, FERAGHAN. 1.90×1.25 m., beginning of the nineteenth century. Private collection, Teheran

8   Persia, KASHAN (or ARDEBIL). Private collection, Teheran

9   Persia, KHORASAN. 1.90×1.25 m., 5 knots per sq.cm. Private collection, Teheran

10 a, b   Persia, FERAGHAN. 1.90×1.25 m., 6 knots per sq.cm., mid-nineteenth century. Private collection, Teheran

11   Persia, KHORASAN. 1.50×1.00 m., 6 knots per sq.cm., first half of the nineteenth century. Private collection, Teheran

12 a, b   Persia, ISFAHAN. 1.50×2.00 m., beginning of the twentieth century. Private collection, Teheran

13 a, b   Persia, KHORASAN. 1.90×1.25 m., 6 knots per sq.cm., end of the nineteenth century. Private collection, Teheran

14   Persia, SARUK. Mid-nineteenth century. Private collection, Teheran

15 a, b   Persia, TEHERAN. 1.90×1.25 m., 7 knots per sq.cm., end of the nineteenth century. Private collection, Teheran

16 a, b   Persia, JOSHAGHAN. 1.90×1.25 m., 7 knots per sq.cm., end of the nineteenth century. Private collection, Teheran

17   Persia, SHIRAZ. 1.90×1.25 m., 5 knots per sq.cm., mid-nineteenth century. Private collection, Teheran

18   Persia, BIJAR. 1.90×1.25 m., 6 knots per sq. cm., first half of the nineteenth century. Private collection, Teheran

19   Persia, SARUK. 1.90×1.25 m., 8 knots per sq.cm., mid-nineteenth century. Private collection, Teheran

20   Persia. 4.00×0.85 m., end of the nineteenth century. Private collection, Kabul

21 a, b   Persia. Prayer carpet, silk and wool, 8 knots per sq.cm., second half of the eighteenth century. Hall of Forty Pillars, Isfahan

22 a, b   Persia, KASHAN. 1.90×1.25 m., 8 knots per sq.cm., mid-nineteenth century. Private collection, Teheran

23 a, b, c   Persia, SAFAVID. Archaeological Museum, Teheran

24 a, b   Persia, SAFAVID. 1.45×1.00 m., Archaeological Museum, Teheran

25 a, b, c   Persia. Archaeological Museum, Teheran

26   Persia, TABRIZ. 1.30×1.75 m., first half of the nineteenth century. Museum Golestan, Teheran

27   Persia, KHORASAN. 2.20×1.50 m., 6 knots per sq.cm., first half of the nineteenth century. Private collection, Teheran

28 a, b   Persia, TABRIZ. 2.20×1.40 m., 6 knots per sq.cm., first half of the nineteenth century. Private collection, Teheran

29   Persia, FERAGHAN. 1.90×1.25 m., 8 knots per sq.cm., first half of the nineteenth century. Private collection, Teheran

30 a, b   Persia, SARUK. 1.90×1.25 m., 7 knots per sq.cm., mid-nineteenth century. Private collection, Teheran

31   Persia, MALAYER. 1.40×1.90 m., first half of the twentieth century. Museum Golestan, Teheran

32 a, b   Persia, TABRIZ. 1.30×1.70 m., silk, second half of the eighteenth century. Museum Golestan, Teheran

33 a, b   Persia, FERAGHAN. 1.90×1.25 m., 8 knots per sq.cm., first half of the nineteenth century. Private collection, Teheran

34   Persia, KASHGAI. 1.90×1.25 m., 6 knots per sq.cm., second half of the nineteenth century. Private collection, Teheran

35	Persia, TABRIZ. 1.30×1.80 m., beginning of the nineteenth century. Museum Golestan, Teheran
36 a, b, c	Persia, TEHERAN. 1.30×1.90 m., end of the nineteenth century, Museum Golestan, Teheran
37	Persia, Archaeological Museum, Teheran
38	Persia, KERMAN. 1.20×2.00 m., end of the nineteenth century. Museum Golestan, Teheran
39 a, b	Persia, KASHAN. 1.90×1.25 m., 8 knots per sq.cm., mid-nineteenth century. Private collection, Teheran
40	Western Turkestan, BESHIR. 1.80×1.00 m., c. 1900. Private collection, Kabul
41 a, b	Western Turkestan, BOKHARA. 3.25×3.50 m., end of the nineteenth century. Private collection, Kabul
42	Western Turkestan, YOMUD. 1.70×1.00 m., first half of the twentieth century. Private collection, Kabul
43	Western Turkestan, YOMUD. 1.80×1.10 m., mid-twentieth century. Private collection, Kabul
44	Western Turkestan, TEKKE-TURKOMAN. 2.00×3.00 m., 60 knots per sq.cm., second half of the nineteenth century. Private collection, Teheran
45 a, b	Western Turkestan, BESHIR. 1.20×1.10 m., beginning of the twentieth century. Private collection, Kabul
46 a, b	Western Turkestan, YOMUD. 2.20×1.40 m., 60 knots per sq.cm., end of the nineteenth century. Private collection, Teheran
47	Beluchistan. 1.70×1.00 m., beginning of the twentieth century. Private collection, Kabul
48	Western Turkestan, PENDE. 2.00×1.25 m., beginning of the twentieth century. Private collection, Kabul
49 a, b	Beluchistan. 2.00×1.15 m., beginning of the twentieth century. Private collection, Kabul
50	Afghanistan. 1.90×1.40 m. Private collection, Kabul
51 a, b	Asia Minor, KONYA. 3.64×1.40 m., end of the seventeenth century. Private collection, Paris
52 a, b	Asia Minor, KULA. End of the eighteenth century. Private collection, Paris
53	Asia Minor, GHIORDES. 2.15×1.47 m., beginning of the nineteenth century. Private collection, Paris
54	Asia Minor, BERGAMA. 1.48×1.22 m., the seventeenth century. Private collection, Paris
55 a, b	Asia Minor, LADIK. Prayer carpet, 1.85×1.15 m., end of the seventeenth century. Galerie Persane, Paris
56	Asia Minor, BANDIRMA. Prayer carpet, 1.52×1.25 m., beginning of the nineteenth century. Private collection, Paris
57 a, b, c	Asia Minor, KULA. Prayer carpet, 1.78×1.15 m., end of the seventeenth century. Private collection, Paris
58 a, b	Asia Minor, GHIORDES. 1.65×1.15 m., end of the eighteenth century. Galerie Persane, Paris
59	Asia Minor, KULA. 1.98×1.35 m., end of the seventeenth century. Private collection, Paris
60	Asia Minor, USHAK. Prayer carpet, 2.22×1.38 m., end of the seventeenth century. Private collection, Paris
61 a, b	Asia Minor, GHIORDES. 2.15×1.47 m., beginning of the nineteenth century. Private collection, Paris
62 a, b	Caucasus. 1.00×1.50 m., mid-nineteenth century. Museum Golestan, Teheran
63 a, b, c	Caucasus, KUBA. 1.90×1.25 m., mid-nineteenth century. Private collection, Teheran
64 a, b	Caucasus, DERBEND. 1.90×1.25 m., mid-nineteenth century. Private collection, Teheran
65	Caucasus, SHIRVAN. 1.90×1.25 m., mid-nineteenth century. Private collection, Teheran
66 a, b, c	Caucasus, SHIRVAN. 1.90×1.25 m., mid-nineteenth century. Private collection, Teheran
67 a, b	Kurdistan. 1.25×1.90 m., mid-nineteenth century. Museum Golestan, Teheran
68	Kurdistan. 1.90×1.30 m., beginning of the nineteenth century. Museum Golestan, Teheran
69 a, b, c	Kurdistan. 1.90×1.25 m., beginning of the nineteenth century. Private collection, Teheran
70	Kurdistan. 1.30×1.25 m., beginning of the nineteenth century. Museum Golestan, Teheran
71 a, b	Kurdistan. 1.35×2.20 m., beginning of the nineteenth century. Museum Golestan, Teheran
72 a, b	Kurdistan. 1.25×1.90 m., mid-nineteenth century. Museum Golestan, Teheran
73 a, b, c	Kurdistan. 2.30×1.40 m., mid-nineteenth century. Private collection, Teheran
74	Kurdistan. 1.20×1.90 m., mid-nineteenth century. Museum Golestan, Teheran

CENTRES OF CARPET PRODUCTION

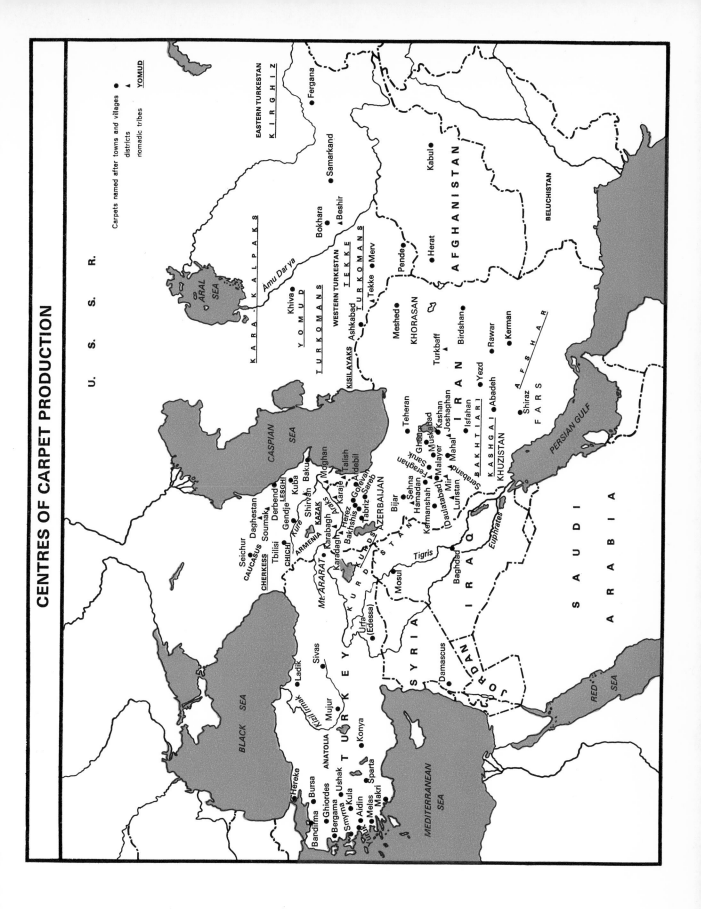

Carpets named after towns and villages ●
districts ▲
nomadic tribes YOMUD

U. S. S. R.

EASTERN TURKESTAN ●
K I R G H I Z

● Fergana

● Samarkand

KARA - KALPAKS

Bokhara ● ● Beshir

● Kabul

A F G H A N I S T A N

BELUCHISTAN

Àmu Dar ya

ARAL SEA

Khiva ●
Y O M U D

WESTERN TURKESTAN
T E K K E
TURKOMANS

Pende ●
● Herat

Ashkabad ▲
KISILAYAKS

Tekke ▲ ● Merv

Meshed ●
KHORASAN
Turkbaff ▲

Birdshan ●
● Rawar
● Kerman
A F S H A R

Yezd ●
Abadeh ●
● Shiraz
F A R S

CASPIAN SEA

Seichur ●
Daghestan
CAUCASUS Soumak ▲
CHERKESS
Tbilisi ●
CHICHI
Derbend ●
Gendje LESGHI
Kuba ●
ARMENIA
Mt. ARARAT

Shirvan ●
Kura
Karabagh ▲
Aras
Karadagh ▲
Bakhshis
Karaje ▲
Herez ●
Tabriz ●
Goevan ●
Sareb ●
AZERBAIJAN

Moghan ▲
Talish ●
Aldebil ●
Baku ●

Teheran ●
Bijar ●
Sehna ●
Hamadan ●
Kefmanshah ●
(Daulatabad) Mir ▲
Luristan
Serabend ▲
BAKHTIARI
KASHGAI
KHUZISTAN

Ghoum ●
Feraghan
Saruk
Malayer ▲
Mahal ▲
Muskabad ▲
Kashan ●
Joshaghan ▲
Isfahan ●

I R A N

Urfa ●
(Edessa)
K U R D S
KURDISTAN
Tigris

Mosul ●

Baghdad ●

I R A Q

Euphrates

Damascus ●

S Y R I A

J O R D A N

S A U D I   A R A B I A

PERSIAN GULF

RED SEA

Sivas ●
Ladik ●
Mujur ●
Kizil Irmak

ANATOLIA
T U R K E Y

Konya ●
Sparta ●
Makri ●
Melas ●
Aidin ●
Kula ●
Smyrna ●
Ushak ●
Ghiordes ●
Bergama ●
Bandirma ●
Bursa ●
Hereke ●
Yuruk

BLACK SEA

MEDITERRANEAN SEA

1 a, b Persia, **DOSAR**
        Whole carpet and detail
2   Persia, **HAMADAN**

4 a, b   Persia, **SARUK**
Whole carpet and detail

7 a, b   Persia, **FERAGHAN**
Whole carpet, detail

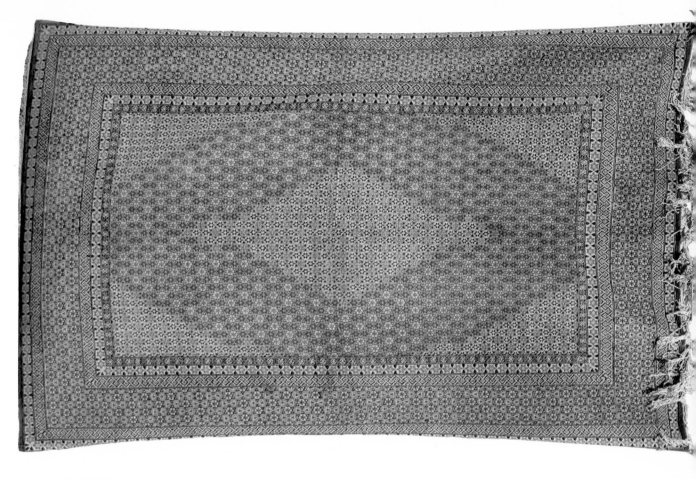

8 Persia, **KASHAN** (or Ardebil)
9 Persia, **KHORASAN**

10 a, b Persia, **FERAGHAN**
        Whole carpet and detail

11   Persia, **KHORASAN**

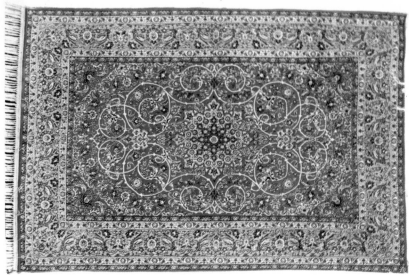

12 a, b Persia, **ISFAHAN**
Whole carpet and detail

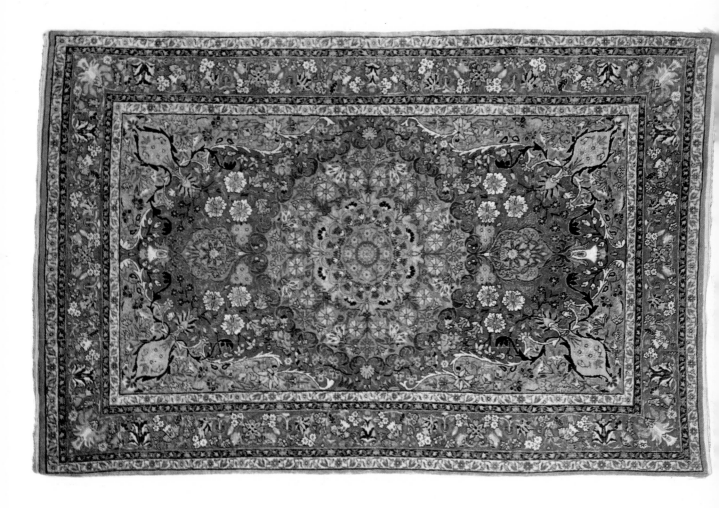

13 a, b Persia, **KHORASAN**
Whole carpet and detail

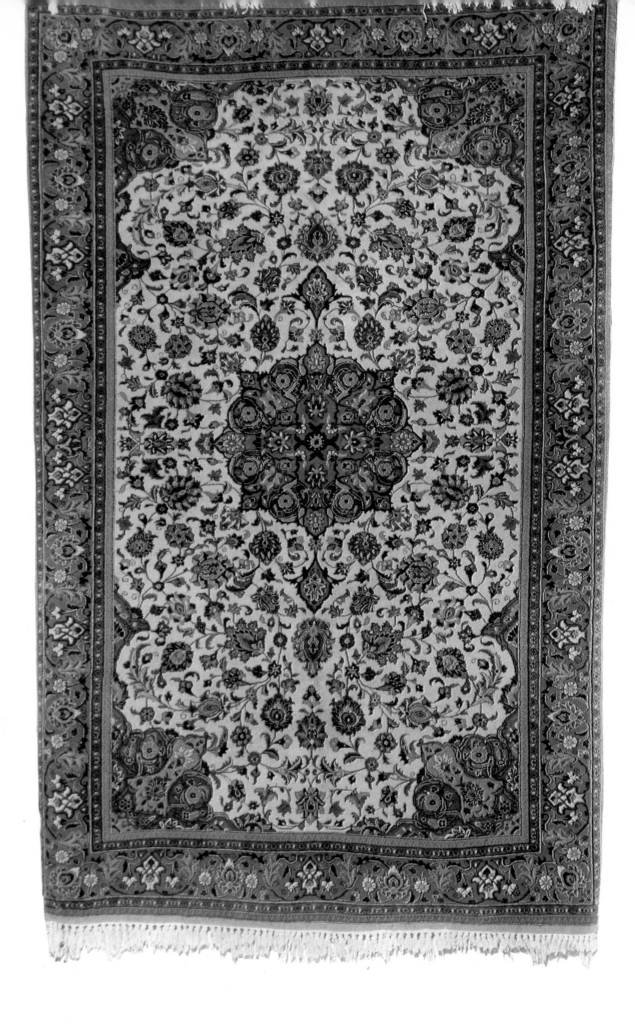

15 a, b   Persia, **TEHERAN**
Whole carpet and detail

16 a, b   Persia, **JOSHAGAN**
Whole carpet and detail

17   Persia, **SHIRAZ**

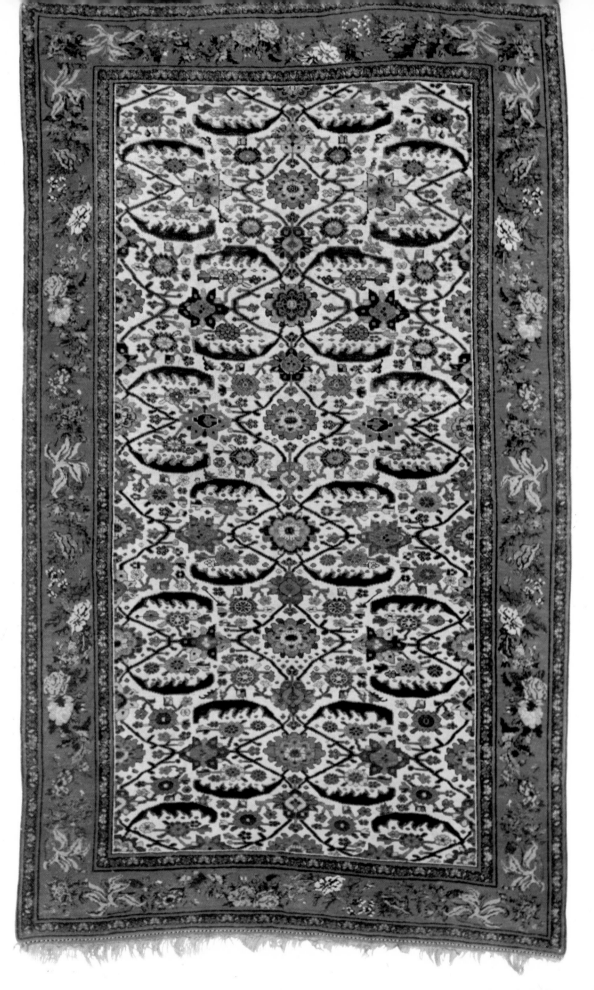

18   Persia,
BIJAR

19 Persia, **SARUK**

20 Persia

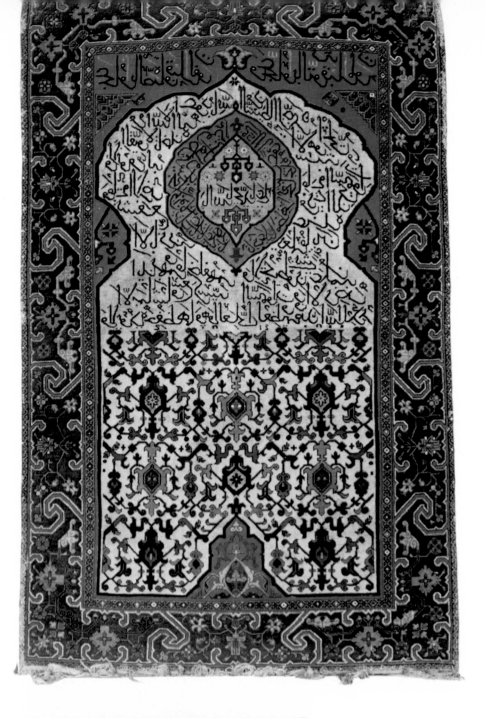

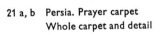
21 a, b Persia. Prayer carpet
Whole carpet and detail

22 a, b Persia, **KASHAN**
Whole carpet and detail

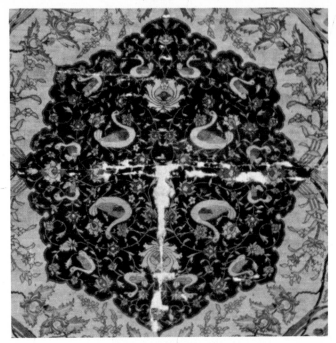

23 a, b, c Persia, **SAFAVID**
Whole carpet
and details

24 a, b   Persia, **SAFAVID**
Whole carpet and detail

25 a, b, c Persia
Whole carpet and details

26 Persia, **TABRIZ**   27 Persia, **KHORASAN**

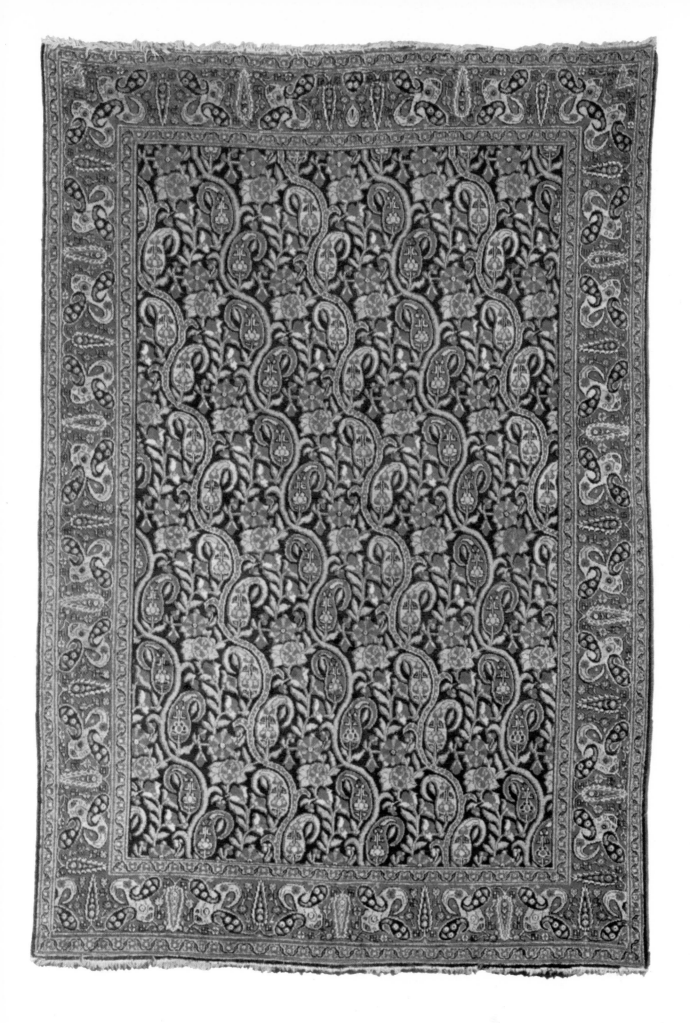

28 a, b Persia, **TABRIZ**
Whole carpet and detail

29 Persia, **FERAGHAN**

30 a, b   Persia, **SARUK**
Whole carpet and detail

31   Persia, **MALAYER**

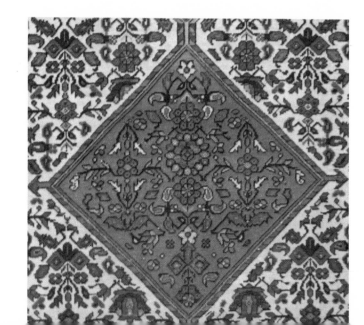

32 a, b   Persia, **TABRIZ**
Whole carpet and detail

34   Persia, **KASHGAI**

35   Persia, **TABRIZ**

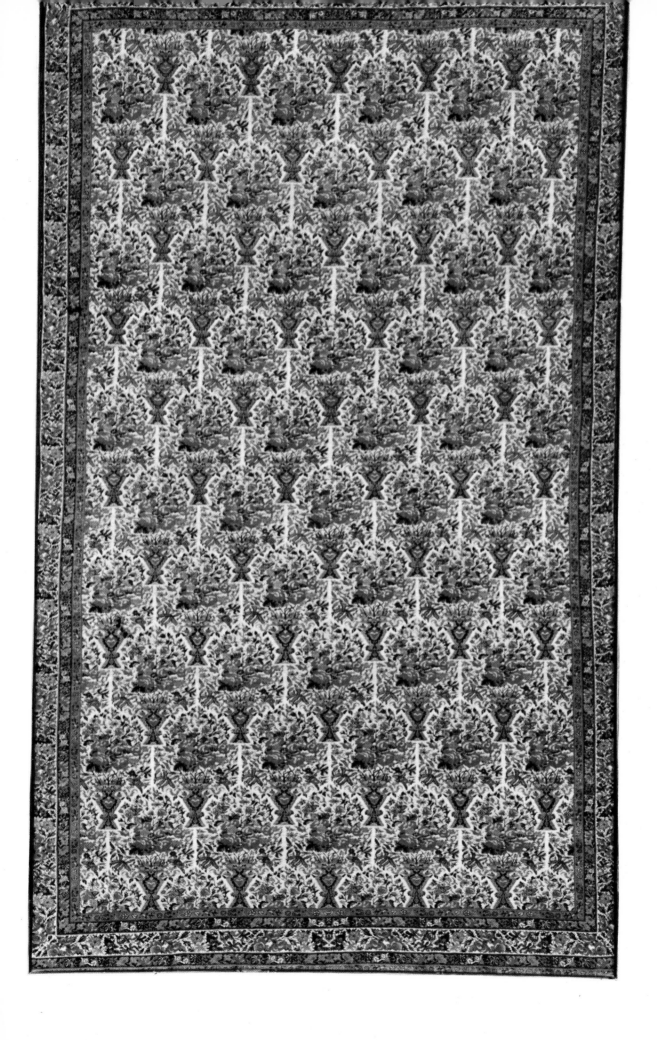

49 a, b   Beluchistan. Whole carpet and detail

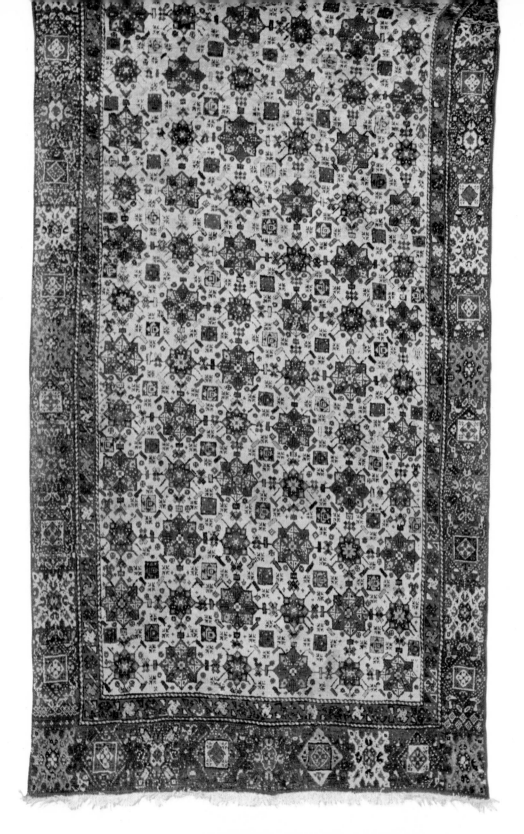

50   Afghanistan

52 a, b   Asia Minor, **KULA**
Whole carpet and detail

53 Asia Minor, **GHIORDES**
54 Asia Minor, **BERGAMA**

55 a, b   Asia Minor, **LADIK.** Prayer carpet
Whole carpet and detail

56 Asia Minor, **BANDIRMA.** Prayer carpet

57 a, b, c   Asia Minor, **KULA.** Prayer carpet
Whole carpet and details

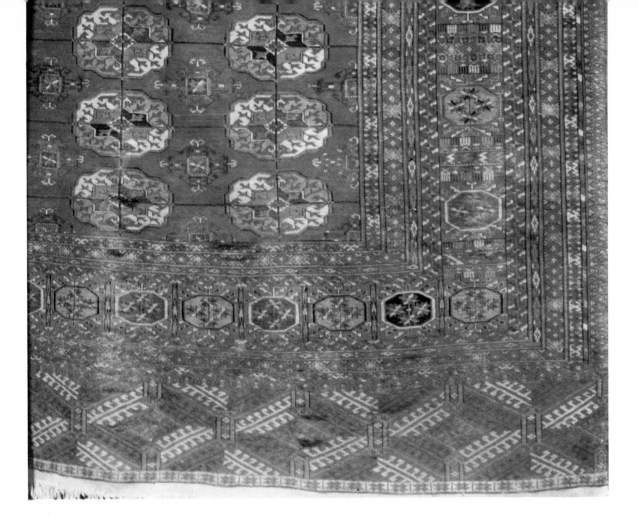

40   Western Turkestan, **BESHIR**
41 a, b   Western Turkestan, **BOKHARA**
       Details

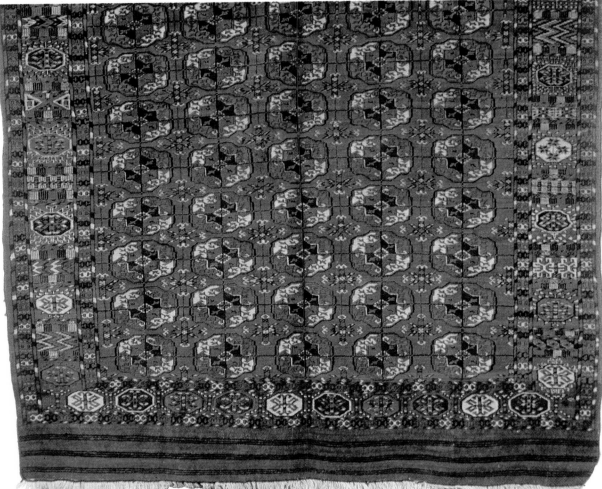

42 Western Turkestan, **YOMUD**

43 Western Turkestan, **YOMUD**

44 Western Turkestan, **TEKKE-TURKOMAN.** Detail

45 a, b   Western Turkestan, **BESHIR**
Whole carpet and detail

46 a, b Western Turkestan, **YOMUD**
Whole carpet and detail

47 Beluchistan
48 Western Turkestan, **PENDE**

58 a, b　Asia Minor, **GHIORDES**
　　　　Whole carpet and detail

59　　　Asia Minor, **KULA**

60 Asia Minor, **USHAK.** Prayer carpet

61 a, b Asia Minor, **GHIORDES**
Whole carpet and detail

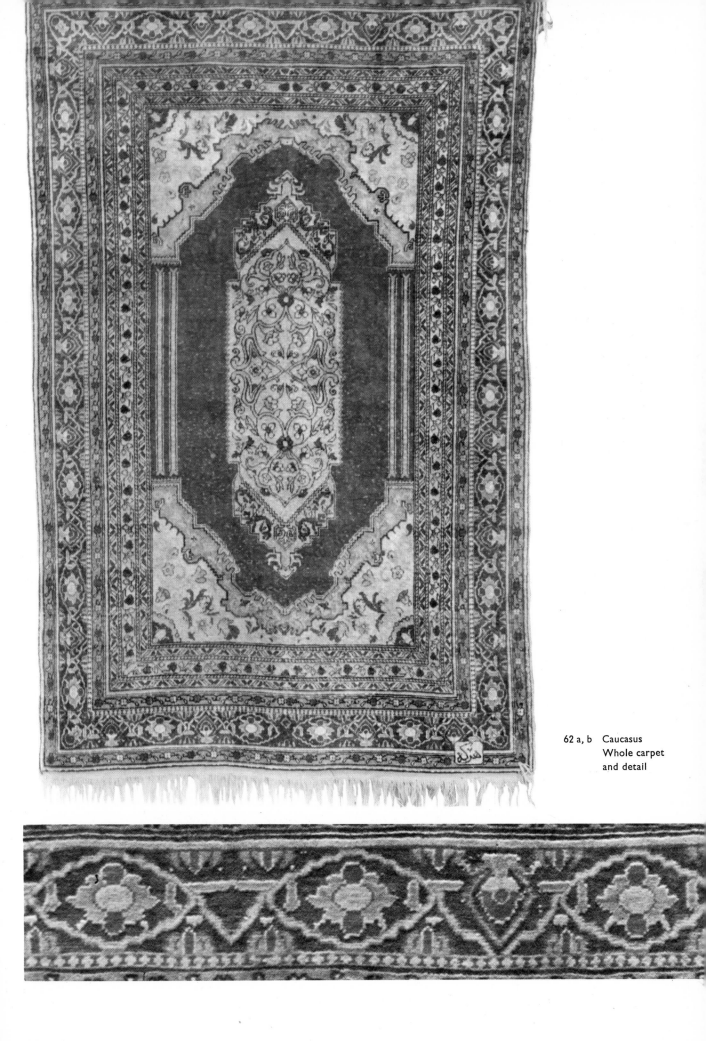

62 a, b Caucasus
Whole carpet
and detail

63 a, b, c   Caucasus, **KUBA**
Whole carpet and details

64 a, b Caucasus, **DERBEND**
Whole carpet and detail

65   Caucasus, **SHIRVAN**

66 a, b, c   Caucasus, **SHIRVAN**
Whole carpet and details

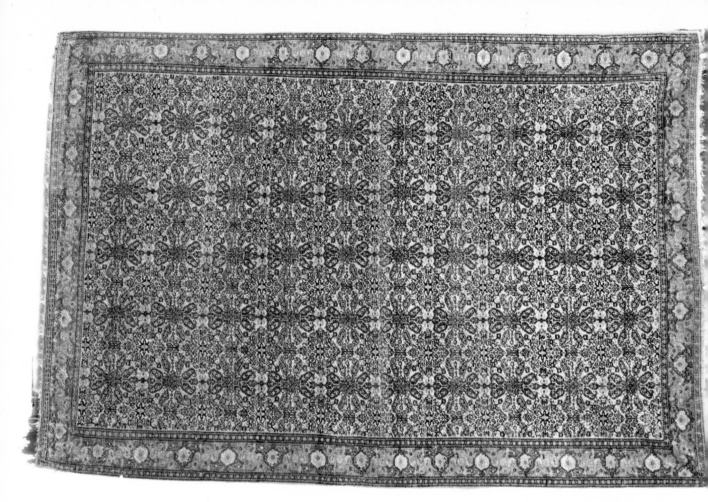

67 a, b   Kurdistan
          Whole carpet and detail
68   Kurdistan

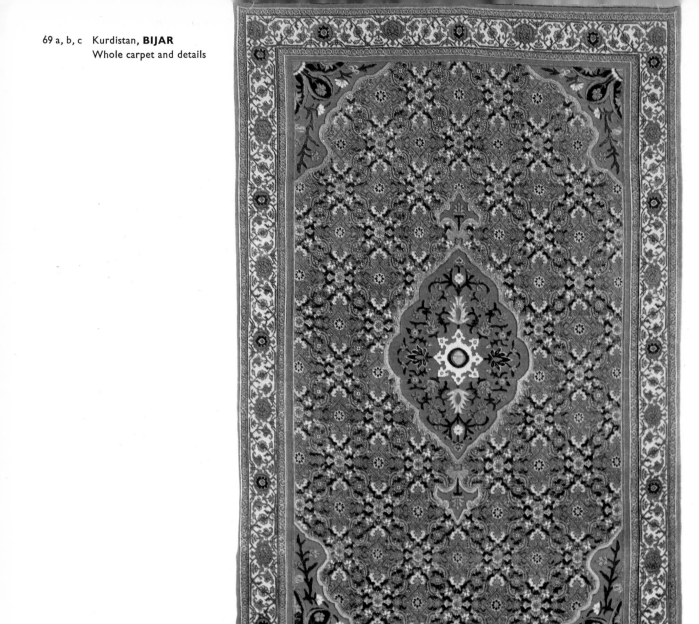

69 a, b, c Kurdistan, **BIJAR**
Whole carpet and details

70 Kurdistan

71 a, b Kurdistan
Whole carpet
and detail

72 a, b Kurdistan
Whole carpet
and detail

73 a, b, c Kurdistan
Whole carpet
and details

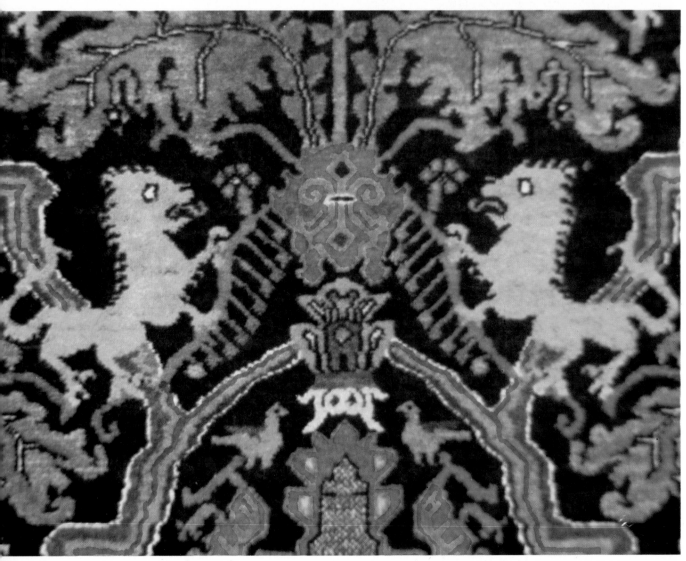

74 Kurdistan